DISCOVERING HOW TO PRAY

Also by Hope MacDonald

Discovering the Joy of Obedience
When Angels Appear
The Flip Side of Liberation (1990)

DISCOVERING HOW TO PRAY

Hope MacDonald

with Study Guide by Dan MacDonald

ZondervanPublishingHouse
Academic and Professional Books
Grand Rapids, Michigan

A Division of HarperCollins*Publishers*

DISCOVERING HOW TO PRAY

Requests for information should be addressed to:
Zondervan Publishing House
Grand Rapids, Michigan 49530

Library of Congress Cataloging-in-Publication Data

MacDonald, Hope.
Discovering how to pray / Hope MacDonald : [with] study guide by Dan MacDonald.
p. cm.
Includes bibliographical references.
ISBN 0-310-28361-2
1. Prayer—Christianity. I. MacDonald, Dan, 1950–
II. Title.
BV210.2.M28 1990
248.3′2—dc20 89–77247
CIP

Printed in the United States of America

92 93 94 95 96 / AK / 7 6 5 4 3

Dedicated to my beloved husband
Harry M. MacDonald
for his constant faith in
Jesus Christ
and
his abiding love for me.

CONTENTS

ACKNOWLEDGMENTS

I would like to express my thanks to the following friends who prayed faithfully for me during the writing of this book. They are:

Jewel Arata
Patty Bylsma
Sue Costin
Cathy Jacobson
Nancy Kandel
Anne MacDonald
Marilyn Mead
Beverly Miller
Beverly Moore
Jay Nelson
Judy Penfield
Dee Sprague
Ruth Starr
Patty Taylor

FROM THE AUTHOR...

In the years since *Discovering How to Pray* was first published, I have received many requests to include a Bible study guide in the book. The enclosed study guide has been used by hundreds of people in study groups on campuses, in Sunday school classes, in home Bible studies, and as a personal Bible study tool or as a one-on-one study guide for discipling. Invariably one word has been used to describe this study guide—"Life-changing."

My prayer for each of you who uses this study guide is that you, too, will find it a "life-changing" experience in your walk with the Lord Jesus.

FOREWORD

Some people think there are already enough books about prayer, but I believe God continues to bring forth His truths in ever-new thoughts and voices.

In this practical little book on prayer, Hope MacDonald shares new insights and ideas on a much-neglected aspect of our Christian experience—our prayer and devotional life. I don't believe there is a Christian today who does not long to have a more meaningful prayer life.

This book gives you simple guidelines that can fill your prayer life with power and meaning. It is a book you will want to keep and refer to from time to time through the years. You will want to share it with others and use it as a study guide in small groups. You will find, as I did, that you will not be able to put it down until you have finished it.

Thank God for another good book on prayer!

Rosalind Rinker

LORD, TEACH ME HOW TO PRAY!

"The saints and mystics, we know, have learned how to hear the voice of the will of God in stillness, how to pass from mere words to the prayer of silence, how to become brave enough to pray the prayer that reaches and shares pain. But the directions they give from high up on the ladder of prayer are not much help to those of us who are still stumbling about down below. What we need are instructions as to how to begin where we are now—at the beginning—and this is just what this book does for us.

DISCOVERING HOW TO PRAY is a practical book and a happy one. How could it be anything else when prayer is our way to God who is the fullness of all joy?"

—Elizabeth Goudge
author of *GREEN DOLPHIN STREET*
and *A CHILD FROM THE SEA*

ONE

LEARNING TO PRAY

I remember the first time I asked God to teach me to pray. We had just arrived in Brazil as missionaries. My daughter, Debbie, and I were having our first experience shopping at the feira, the open-air market. The streets were hot and dusty and filled with hundreds of busy shoppers, all chattering in their own language. The small, covered stands were filled with strange-looking fruits and vegetables. My first purchase was a piece of fruit called mamaõ. As I held out my faded, wrinkled money to the vendor (hoping he would be honest enough to take just the price of the fruit), I suddenly felt reduced to the state of a two-year-old. Here I was, a fairly intelligent mother of three children, and I couldn't even give the man the right amount of money! My vocabulary consisted of three phrases: *good morning, good evening,* and *thank you.* The people were pushing and shoving around us, trying to get a good look at the "foreigners." I felt so helpless.

My eyes filled with tears of frustration as I took Debbie's hand and walked to the next little stand. I wondered what we were doing there. How could we ever learn the language well enough to communicate God's great love to the students? And it was there, as I stood in front of the comforting, familiar green-bean stand, that I cried out, "O, Lord, teach me to pray!" I knew then anything we would accomplish in the land of Brazil would only be done through the power of prayer, and I didn't know much about it.

God heard the prayer I whispered to Him in the crowded Brazilian marketplace, and He began to teach me how to pray. That was eleven years ago, and today I find myself sharing with you the nine steps that have changed my prayer life.

I have since found that I was not alone in my quest. In talking to Christians around the world, I have discovered that their greatest desire is to know how to pray. When a survey was conducted on "Sermons Americans want to hear," it was discovered that the people's first choice was "How can I make prayer more effective?"[1] Recently, our pastor announced he would be speaking on prayer the following Sunday. The next week the church was packed. They had to bring in extra chairs. When he stood up to speak, there was a hushed atmosphere of expectancy. I noticed people all around me reaching for paper and pencil so they could write down ideas that would help them become praying Christians. Christians want to pray, but they don't seem to know how. Our spiritual lives are at a low ebb.

A few weeks ago a troubled teenage boy was talking to my son Dan about this same thing. He said, "I know I should spend time with God each day, and I really do

---

[1] See *Prayer—Conversing with God* by Rosalind Rinker (Grand Rapids: Zondervan, 1975) for discussion on group prayer.

want to. I read my Bible for twenty minutes, and then when I pray I say everything I can think of in two minutes. Can you help me?"

His plea reminded me so much of what the disciples asked Jesus when they came to Him one afternoon and said, "Master, teach us to pray." As you read through the Gospels, you will find that this is the only thing they ever asked Jesus to teach them. They had watched His life and knew prayer was an important part of every great and significant moment. They knew Jesus didn't pray just to set a good example for them, but because it made a difference in His life. They saw that He *expected* it to make a difference. And because they saw Him pray so often, they asked Him to teach them to pray. If you feel the way I often do, as though you do not know how to pray the way you would like to, don't be discouraged. You're in good company. Even the disciples had to ask Jesus to teach them to pray!

A few months ago when my husband and I were in Korea, he was talking about prayer with the pastor of one of the largest churches in the city of Seoul. At the end of their conversation, the pastor shook his head sadly and said, "The greatest need of my people is to know how to pray." That same evening we went to a coffeehouse where we talked to some students about prayer. One of the girls remarked, "I have been a Christian for eleven years, but I do not know how to pray. I wish I did." A few weeks later, I was speaking to a group of women in the Philippines. When I finished, they crowded around me saying how often they longed for a meaningful prayer life, but they just didn't know how to go about it. This same thought has been expressed to my husband and myself over and over again as we have talked to

Christians in Australia, India, and other parts of the world.

The question then arises, What exactly is prayer? Is it really so complicated that Christians must spend a lifetime searching for it? Or have we made something confusing out of what God intended to be beautiful in its simplicity?

I like to think of prayer as a conversation between two friends who love and understand each other. It is through prayer that we see God's love and power at work in our lives and in the lives of the people for whom we are praying. As a result, prayer makes us come alive spiritually. We find a new hunger and thirst to spend time with Him and to stay close to Him. Prayer is the key that opens the door to a whole new world—a world lived in the active, conscious presence of the living God. It becomes the foundation of everything we do. Jesus Christ died on the cross to make this communication possible!

You may not understand everything about prayer. I haven't met anyone yet who has all the answers. But we do know one thing *for sure:* When we pray, we see great things happen for God, and when we don't pray, we don't see much happen.

I like to compare prayer to the wind. You cannot actually *see* the wind, but you can see the results of it. Right now as I am writing this, we are having a windstorm. Our baby aspen trees are being bent down almost to the ground. I am seeing the force and power of the wind, but I am not seeing the wind. No one has ever seen it. Yet on a warm summer evening, you can take a walk and feel the gentle breeze against your face. So it is with prayer. You can't capture it and put it under a microscope and say, "Ah, this is what prayer is," but you can see the results of it in your own life and in the lives of those around you.

God has given us prayer that we might draw close to Him, that we might share our lives with Him, and that we might see the miracle of answered prayer each day of our lives. Stop and think for a minute: How long has it been since you've seen a miracle in your life? If it's been longer than a week, that's too long. We believe in a supernatural God—a God who *loves* to do miracles. Are you expecting any miracles in your life today? Look at the life of Jesus during His public ministry. Three-fourths of it was spent doing miracles. This was His way of showing that He is a God of miracles—He is a supernatural God. I think today we have robbed God of His supernatural being. We want to make Him like us, finite and natural. But the God of the Bible is supernatural and infinite. He is a God who moves in history in big ways in response to big prayers. Never forget the wonder of your God or the wonder of your salvation!

This past summer I was speaking to a group of university students. When I finished, I opened the meeting for questions. One boy asked me a question that is usually asked every time I talk on prayer. He said, "Why should I pray? Won't God answer my prayers whether I pray or not?" My answer to that is no. "Doesn't God want to save the whole world?" Yes, but *through you!* If you are a Christian today, it is only because someone cared enough for you to tell you about the love of Jesus.

There is a story I want to share with you to illustrate this point. The story begins with Jesus returning to heaven after the Resurrection. Can you imagine the "welcome home" party the angels had planned for Him?

They had a banquet table spread with everything He liked best. (Much like we do when our children return home from college or for a visit.) After they had finished eating, the angels leaned back on their cushions and asked Jesus to tell them all about His experiences on earth. He told them how He walked the dusty roads, healed the sick, and raised the dead. He told them how He died on the cross to pay the penalty for our sin and how He rose again on the third day. When He finished, there was a hushed silence. Then one of the angels said, "And now, Lord, is it our turn? Will we be able to go down to earth and tell the people the marvelous thing You have done for them?" And the Lord shook His head and replied, "No." At this the angels were greatly puzzled and asked, "How then are You going to get this wonderful message to all the people of the earth?" And Jesus answered, "I have left it in the hands of eleven fishermen." Then the angels said, "But, Lord—what if they fail?" And Jesus said, "I have no other plan."

You see, God has chosen to limit Himself to working through us! He has made us His partners and entrusted the lost and dying world into our care. "Apart from us He has no body in the world, no hands and feet and heart and voice to bring God's mercy to a suffering world."[2]

Yes, God wants to save the whole world, but He will only accomplish it through you. And, yes, God wants to answer prayer, but He doesn't *unless we pray*. All God wants to do in this world through you can only be done

---

[2]Elizabeth Goudge, *The Joy of the Snow* (New York: Coward, McCann and Geoghegan, Inc., 1974), p. 242.

through prayer. This is the one condition that must be met.

Why should we pray? Because God answers prayer. Do we really believe that? Do we *live* as though we believe it? If we did, I think we would all be spending more time on our knees in prayer. Our time with God would be the most important thing we did all day. Unfortunately, most of us do not live this way. Year after year we pray our little prayers and get our little answers. We wonder why we see so little being accomplished for Jesus in our lives and in the world. Where are the big prayers like the ones prayed by men such as Hudson Taylor, Jonathan Goforth, George Müller, and Andrew Murray? If you want to read some faith-building books, read the life stories of these men and see how they prayed. They prayed big prayers, and they expected and got big answers. I like what St. Theresa of Avila said, "You pay God a compliment by asking great things of Him."

And the only way we are ever going to learn to pray is by *doing* it. We can read all the books that have ever been written about prayer, but until we actually choose, by an act of our will, to pray, we will never learn. Many years ago I saw these words written above a library entrance: "He who reads and reads and never does is like a farmer who plows and plows and never reaps."

In the following chapters, I would like to share with you nine basic steps that can help your prayer life become more meaningful. I hope you will take these steps and make them a part of your life. The outline in the back of the book you can tear out and keep in a handy place. I hope you will use it to teach yourself and others how to pray, for this book is not written for the person who knows how to pray. It is written for the one who wants to learn.

STUDY GUIDE

1. What is the author's definition of prayer?
2. Look at these four important words in the definition. What aspects of prayer do these words describe?
   Conversation
   Friends
   Love
   Understand
3. Write your own definition of prayer.
4. Give several reasons, *not* benefits, for why you should pray.
5. What are the benefits or blessings you receive through prayer? List several from the chapter, as well as any others you can think of.
6. Prayerlessness has been considered a sin. In light of your previous answers, why do you think this is true?
7. The author acknowledges that prayer is something with which we all struggle. Why is it often difficult for us to pray (Eph. 6:10–12)?
8. Why can it be difficult for you to pray? What or who keeps you from praying? I suggest you keep a list of your reasons. As you continue through this study, notice how many of these problem areas are mentioned.
9. The author hints at two essentials for beginning and maintaining a quality prayer life. To understand these, answer the following questions:

a. What does the author realize and admit as a result of her experience at the feiřa in Brazil? How does this relate to the first beatitude in the Sermon on the Mount (Matt. 5:3)?

b. According to the author, what is the only way you will ever learn to pray?

c. How do these two principles relate to what Paul expresses about the Christian life in Philippians 2:12–14?

10. How does the author answer the commonly-asked question, "Does prayer really make a difference?"

11. For further study, read the following verses and answer each question.

a. Can prayer make a difference in the life of the one who prays?

Ps. 118:5–6	Dan. 9:20–23	Phil. 4:6–8
Ps. 138:3	Joel 2:32	James 1:2–6
Lam. 3:57	Luke 11:13	1 John 1:9

b. Can prayer make a difference in the lives of those for whom you pray?

2 Chron. 7:14	Phil. 1:9–11	1 Thess. 3:10–13
Eph. 1:18–19	Col. 1:9–12	2 Thess. 1:11–12
Eph. 3:16–21	2 Tim. 1:3	2 Thess. 2:16–17
Heb. 13:20–21		

c. Can prayer make a difference in the physical world?

1 Chron. 4:10	Matt. 6:11	James 5:13–18
Ps. 65:2, 5	Prov. 30:7–9	Acts 16:25–26

d. Can prayer make a difference in God's work of redemption throughout the world?

Matt. 6:10	Acts 1:13–14	Matt. 9:36–38
John 17:9–11; 15–21	Eph. 6:19–20	Rev. 3:20–21
	Col. 4:2–6	

TWO

ARROW PRAYERS

England is a country where archery is still practiced. You can drive through the small villages and see large targets set up in the clearings of the woods. It is a precision skill that is fascinating to watch. The archer pulls back on the bow until the string is taut and then lets the arrow fly swiftly and faultlessly through the air to its target.

In this book I will be talking about two kinds of prayer. One is what I call an "arrow prayer." The second is the prayer of worship and intercession. It is the second one to which I will devote most of this book.

But first of all, what is an arrow prayer? It is the kind of prayer we shoot up to God all day long. It is the natural turning to God throughout the day—sharing with Him our feelings, our happiness, our hurts and disappointments. An arrow prayer is as spontaneous and natural as breathing. It is the constant awareness of the presence of God. It is the kind of prayer we shoot up to God when we see our husband come home from a hard day at work. His shoulders are drooping and his face is lined with worry. "O God," we pray, "help me to give him the kind of love and understanding he needs." It's sitting on the bed with your teenage daughter, listening as she pours out her problems. Up goes the arrow prayer, "Help, Lord, I need wisdom to know what to say to her." It's talking on the phone to a friend who has a heartbreaking story. You can't think of one helpful or comforting thing to say, so while she talks you shoot up an arrow that says, "Lord, tell me what you would say if You were talking to her." These are arrow prayers, and we're shooting them up to heaven every day of our lives.

The Bible tells us we are to pray without ceasing (1 Thess. 5:17). What does this mean? Does it mean we should shut ourselves up in a room and do nothing but pray for twenty-four hours? No, it means we should be in an *attitude* of prayer all day. When we get up in the morning, we say, "Good morning, Lord. Thank You for the night's rest and for another day in which to live for You." While you fix breakfast or clean house, drive to work or walk to school, you're shooting up little arrow prayers, thanking Him for specific things or asking for His help and strength.

Stonewall Jackson was a man of arrow prayers. He said, "I have so fixed the habit in my mind that I never raise a glass of water to my lips without asking God's blessing, never seal a letter without putting a word of prayer under the seal, never take a letter from the post without a brief sending of my thoughts heavenward, never change my classes in the lecture room without a minute's petition for the cadets who go out and for those who come in." Is this the way you go through your day, constantly committing yourself and all you do to the Lord? This is what the Christian life is all about—a moment-by-moment walk with God. He longs for each one of us to have this kind of life.

The other day I was driving down the street when I heard the shrill siren of an ambulance. As I pulled over to the curb to let it pass, I prayed, "Dear Lord, please be with that sick person. Send Your healing power into his life, and may he be aware that You are with him. If he does not know You, may Your Holy Spirit bring to his mind any truth he may have heard about You during his life. Bring him into Your family, I pray."

There are so many opportunities to pray for others during the day. The dignified, elderly lady who passes you on the street—somehow you sense she is lonely and needs to feel the touch of Jesus on her life. The young person who is searching so desperately for some meaning to his life. The businessman in the elevator, with his bulging briefcase and heavy sighs. The newborn baby being pushed in the buggy by her proud, young mother. I never drive by a high school without praying for God to send a Young Life leader, or *someone,* to tell the students about Jesus. When you drive by a church, pray that the minister may be a man of God and that his church will be a place where people can worship and hear the truth.

There is the arrow prayer of thanksgiving when you take the cake out of the oven and it doesn't fall! (If you live above 6,000 feet, that's something!) There is the thankfulness that wells up in your heart when the plane your husband is on lands safely, when your baby's temperature is normal for the first time in three days, when a friend calls on the phone to share some good news, when you receive your sister's happy letter. As you go through your day in this attitude of prayer, you will find yourself saying "Thank You, Jesus" a hundred times for a hundred different things.

These arrow prayers are an important part of our

Christian life, but *we cannot live on them.* They must be grounded upon the foundation of our prayers of worship and intercession. Otherwise, it will be like the husband who gives his wife a little peck on the cheek several times a week, year after year, and then wonders why his marriage isn't growing! The popular thought today is not to get too worried or burdened down with guilt feelings because you are not spending a certain amount of time alone with God in prayer and worship. We're constantly being told, "Don't get all hung up with rules and discipline, or it will take all the freedom from the Christian life." But this is not so. Jesus said, "You will know the truth, and *the truth will set you free*" (John 8:32). If we want to be completely free, we must know the truth. And the only way we are ever going to know the truth is by spending time alone with Jesus Christ, who is Truth.

Nothing is more neglected today in our Christian life than the prayer of worship and intercession. Our lives have become so full of things—coming and going and doing—that we no longer have any time left over to pray. We wonder what became of the joy and the first love we had when we came to know Jesus. We wonder why our hearts are cold and dead spiritually. We wonder why life seems so confused and full of problems without solutions. It's because we have become a generation of prayerless Christians, who in turn are producing prayerless followers.

Read through the Gospels, and you will be amazed, as I was, at how many times it says, "Very early in the morning, while it was still dark, Jesus got up and went off to a solitary place, where he prayed" (Mark 1:35). If

Jesus needed to spend time alone in prayer, how do we possibly think we can get along without it?

Read Mark 1:21–35 and see how busy and active Jesus had been the day before. Yet He made time to rise early and be alone to pray. He knew He would be spending the day ministering to those in need, and He had to be alone with God to be refreshed and renewed spiritually. There was simply no way He could have been ready for a new day of helping and loving others if He had not first departed to a quiet place and prayed. We, too, need to have our lives renewed and refreshed daily if we're going to be shining lights in the lost and dying world that surrounds us. We need to learn what it means to wait upon the Lord in prayer. "They who wait for the LORD shall renew their strength, they shall mount up with wings like eagles, they shall run and not be weary; they shall walk and not faint" (Isa. 40:31).

Jesus spent the whole night in prayer before choosing His disciples. I wonder what would happen if we spent a night in prayer before making an important decision?

As Christians living in a troubled world, we need both kinds of prayer in our lives. We need the arrow prayer and we need the quiet time of prayer, alone with God, in worship and intercession. In the following chapters we will deal with the nine steps involved in learning to pray.

STUDY GUIDE

1. Define and describe arrow prayers.
2. How does this type of prayer fit with the definition of prayer in chapter 1?
3. How will praying arrow prayers make 1 Thessalonians 5:17 become a reality for you each day?

4. What does the potentiality of arrow prayers tell you about God's promises?
5. In what ways will God be more accessible for you moment-by-moment if you pray arrow prayers?
6. List some other benefits of "shooting up" arrow prayers.
7. Are arrow prayers insufficient in themselves? Why? What type of prayer should be the foundation of your prayer life?
8. Define a prayer of worship and intercession.
9. The author gives one example of the difference between arrow prayers and prayers of worship and intercession. Can you think of any other examples (John 14:12–15)? Explain how your examples contrast and illustrate the importance of both types of prayer.
10. The Bible often tells us "to wait on God" in reference to prayers of worship and intercession. Examine the following verses carefully to discover in what areas you should wait on God and how your waiting will affect your walk with God.

Ps. 62:1	Ps. 27:14	Isa. 40:31
1 Tim. 6:14, 15	Ps. 25:21	Ps. 40:1–3
Hos. 12:6	Acts 1:4	

THREE

STEP ONE: MAKE TIME TO PRAY

A few weeks ago, I was talking about the prayer of worship and intercession to a group of young Christian leaders. I asked how many spent an hour a day in prayer. Not one hand went up. "Are there any who spend half an hour in prayer?" Two hands went up. "How about fifteen minutes?" I asked. A little over half of them raised their hands. When I asked how many spent five minutes a day in prayer, most of the rest raised their hands. We sat in stunned silence for a few moments as we began to recognize what God had just revealed to each one of us—how little time we spend in prayer.

Why do we pray so little? It isn't that we don't *want* to pray, because I believe most of us do. Maybe it's because we try to sandwich our time with God in between all of our other activities. We try to fit Him into our schedule rather than fitting our schedule around Him.

How much time do you spend in prayer each day? I'm not talking about arrow prayers. I'm talking about the prayer of worship and intercession—the time you *set aside* each day to be alone with God.

The first step on the learning to pray ladder is: We

must make time to pray. We are never going to wake up in the morning and say, "Oh, good! I have time to pray today." It just doesn't happen that way. At least it doesn't with me. Our lives are so full of activities—working, taking care of children, studying at school, serving the Lord, etc.—there just doesn't seem to be any time left over to pray. That's the problem. We're looking for "leftover" time to give to God. We're asking ourselves, "How little can I get by with in my prayer life?" rather than, "How much can I give to God in prayer?" Somehow, we have gotten our priorities confused.

It boils down to, "What do I really feel is essential in my life?" Isn't it true that we manage to make time to do the things we really want to do? We make time to drink that cup of coffee in the morning; we make time to read a book, comb our hair, or talk on the phone. (How many hours are spent each week just talking on the phone!) We make time to ski, golf, or play tennis; we make time to eat and we make time to sleep.

Above all, we make time to watch television. Even if you are one of those people who say, "Oh, I *never* watch television," I would challenge you to keep a record for one week and see how much time you really do watch it. Keep a paper and pencil on top of your television set and write down the amount of time you watch it. Even if you do nothing but look at the news for half an hour each day, you will spend 3 1/2 hours watching TV during the week. Do you spend 3 1/2 hours alone with God in prayer during the week? I remember when I tried this little experiment. I was always one of those who said, rather self-righteously, "I hardly ever watch television." But when I kept a record of one week's viewing, I discovered that I had watched:

one movie (two hours)
one documentary (one hour)
two nights of Billy Graham (two hours)
three half-hour shows on Saturday evening (1½ hours)
the news every night before going to bed (3½ hours)

For one who didn't watch much television, I found I had spent ten hours watching it that week! I can assure you I had not spent ten hours alone with God in prayer that same week!

I am learning that one of the greatest sins we commit against ourselves and those around us is the sin of not praying. Did you ever think of not praying as sin? I didn't until just recently. We all know we should pray and yet so few of us do. The Bible tells us, "Remember that if a man knows what is right and fails to do it, his failure is a real sin" (James 4:17 PHILLIPS). A Christian living a prayerless life is robbed of all the power God intends him to have. Our prayerless lives are the sin that keeps the world from knowing Jesus! They are the sin that keeps us from knowing Him!

You may ask, "How can I make prayer a part of my life?" Ask God to create within you a hunger and thirst to be with Him. He will. "Blessed are those who hunger and thirst for righteousness, *for they will be filled*" (Matt. 5:6, italics mine). This is a promise from God we can claim with assurance.

Have you ever stopped to wonder what the devil's favorite word might be? I've thought a lot about this and have come to the conclusion that his favorite word is *tomorrow*. He is always trying to keep us from praying today. In fact, that must be one of his main jobs—to keep all Christians off their knees. He knows we already belong to God and there is nothing he can do about that. But he can do everything in his power to keep us from becoming effective, believing, praying Christians. *He* knows the power God has made available to us through prayer, and he does everything he can to keep us from it. He is always saying to me, "You can pray tomorrow, Hope. You're so busy today." And when tomorrow comes, he says, "Pray tomorrow." It's always "tomorrow" with the devil, isn't it? Tomorrow—and the next day—and the one following, until we reach the end of our lives and find we have missed much that God had been waiting to give to us.

I remember what Martin Luther said when he was faced with an especially busy day. He said, "I'm so busy today I must spend the first three hours in prayer!" How different from what we say: "I'm so busy today, I'll have to pray tomorrow!" Our priorities are so different from those of men like Moses, David, the apostles, Martin Luther, and all the people whom God has been able to work through in a mighty way. When you read about their lives, you find they all had this one thing in common: the central priority in their lives was prayer.

To pray well, we must make time to pray. We must set aside a time for prayer each day. We should try to make it as regular as possible because we all work better when we are on some sort of schedule. I know I breathe a sigh of relief when summer is over and the children go back to school. It isn't that I don't love my children dearly or thoroughly enjoy the summer—it's just that I seem to function better within the framework of a schedule. Everyone in the house seems to do better.

Our physical bodies are the same. They work best

when we eat at regular times each day and when we go to bed at night at a regular hour.

In the same way, we find our spiritual lives work best when we have a regular time to be alone with God each day, reading His Word and praying.

Look through your daily schedule and find the best time for you to pray. For some people, it's in the early morning. This is certainly the ideal time. But I'll tell you this, the hours between five and seven A.M. are definitely not my husband's best hours. He is a slow starter in the morning, becomes more alert as the day goes on, and is going strong late at night. If he is going to give God his *best time,* it has to be after his morning exercises, shower, and breakfast. When he is all dressed and ready to leave for work, then he goes down to our guest room to be alone with God in prayer.

I have a friend who teaches school. She has a full schedule and has found the best time for her to pray is during lunch hour. She drives to a little park near the school, sits out under a tree, and prays. If it's raining she sits in her car.

If you're a young mother with small children, you probably will have to wait until the children take their naps before you can find fifteen minutes to kneel down in fairly uninterrupted prayer.

In whatever situation we find ourselves, if we do not have at least fifteen minutes out of twenty-four hours to give to God in quiet prayer, then there is something wrong with our schedules. We are either much busier than God wants us to be or our priorities are not in their proper order.

Remember this: Our highest calling in life is not in serving Jesus, but in being *with Him.* He chose twelve disciples that they might be *with Him.* Our effective service and love for others can only come from being alone with God in prayer and in fellowship and in the reading of His Word.

I have a friend who is teaching seven Bible studies a week plus trying to be a good homemaker, loving wife, and devoted mother! Think of the preparation and prayer that must go into those seven studies, besides the actual time spent in teaching. Then think of the hours involved each day in just trying to be a good wife and mother, to say nothing of the time it takes to be a fairly decent homemaker. My friend soon found she was trying to live on her arrow prayers and they weren't enough—they never are. We can get along a few days on arrow prayers—and there are times in life when we may have to—but we can't *live* on them. There is not enough spiritual food in them to keep us alive.

Everything my friend was involved in was good, but what was the *best?* Jesus said the best was being alone with Him each day in prayer.

I like the story of Mary and Martha in the New Testament (Luke 10:38–42). Remember when Jesus went to their home one day for dinner? Martha was busy rushing around the kitchen, trying to get things ready. Mary was simply sitting at the feet of Jesus. Martha couldn't understand this and went into the living room to complain to Jesus, "Do You think it's fair for Mary to be sitting there with You when I have so much work to do?" And Jesus said to her gently, "Martha, Martha—there is really only one thing worth being concerned about, and Mary has discovered it." Have you learned, as Mary did, what is really of lasting value in your life?

No matter how busy and full your day may be, the

most worthwhile thing you can do is to sit alone at the feet of Jesus. Sitting means taking time to be relaxed. Mary didn't go rushing hurriedly into the presence of Jesus with a lot of urgent things she wanted Him to do for her and then rush out again. No, she took time out in the midst of all she had to do, to sit down at His feet. She chose God's best for her life. She made time to *cherish* Him. I have a feeling that after dinner, Mary washed the dishes and cleaned up the kitchen so Martha could learn the joy of sitting at the feet of Jesus.

We need to be reminded of the fact that the Christian life is a life of discipline and obedience. We hear so much today about its being a life of love and freedom. And that is certainly true. But there are two sides to every coin. One side of Christian living is love and freedom, and the other side is discipline and obedience. We cannot separate them.

It seems the word *discipline* is fast disappearing from our vocabulary, and has long since disappeared from our Christian lives. Jesus said, "If anyone would come after me, he must deny himself and take up his cross daily and follow me" (Luke 9:23). Sometimes I think we're great ones for taking up our crosses and following Him. This puts us out where the action is, and that's where we all want to be. But how hard it is to find people who will deny *themselves*. We don't really know too much about denying or disciplining ourselves, do we?

Last winter, my husband and I were in Katmandu, Nepal. It is a fascinating city sprawled at the foot of the great Himalayan Mountains. We spent three days with a nineteen-year-old student named Puskar, who lives with his family in a small village outside of town. His father is a Brahman-Hindu, which is the highest of all the Hindu castes. Every morning at four thirty he would get up and walk barefoot to the next village, which was three miles away. He was going to the temple to pray. The road was narrow, winding, and dark, and it was always foggy that high up in the mountains. When he arrived, before going inside, he would have to bathe in the cold, dirty river that flowed past the temple. After praying in the temple for *an hour,* he would start the long walk back along the mountain road. He would arrive home in time for a cup of very black coffee and then start his full day of work. This was the discipline and dedication of a man who worshiped a false god.

As we listened to Puskar tell us the story of his father's devotion, we were filled with shame. We couldn't help thinking of the weak excuses we so often give for not praying. We find it difficult to roll out of our warm beds onto a soft carpet to pray! Think how few of us would ever pray if we had to walk in the cold and fog for three miles to some empty, dark temple—to say nothing of having to first bathe in a dirty, cold river! We have become a generation of soft, weak, undisciplined, prayerless Christians. Spiritual discipline is the key to the Christian life. It is the only key that will open the door to a full and joyous life with Christ.

Why are there so many weak, frail, stumbling Christians today? Because we have ignored the *only* Source of our strength and power—Jesus Christ—and the importance of being with Him, loving Him, and sharing our lives with Him in prayer.

STUDY GUIDE

1. It's time for true confessions. Think honestly for a moment. How much quality prayer time, not arrow prayer time, do you have each week?

2. How much time do you think is necessary to develop a growing relationship with God? Be realistic!
3. How much time do you spend doing things that are really unnecessary and unimportant? Divide a piece of paper in half. On one side, list your current priorities according to how you spend your time, or what you make time to do. On the other side, list your ideal or hoped for priorities. Notice the comparison. What does it tell you about how you spend your time?
4. According to this chapter, what kind of time do we so often give to God?
5. What is wrong with fitting God into your schedule instead of fitting your schedule around God?
6. What was the first priority in the lives of great people of God?
7. As a Christian, what should be your highest calling in life (Hos. 6:6 LB)? Why? Why isn't serving Jesus the highest calling?
8. Why did Christ offer Himself as a living sacrifice? Because your sins are forgiven, what privilege do you enjoy in your relationship with God?
9. What is the key word in the author's first step of prayer? Why?
10. What motivates you to make anything a part of your life (Matt. 5:6)?
11. To "make time," the author gives you these important and practical ways to begin:
    a. Choose the *best* time for *you*.
    b. Be *consistent* and set a *regular* time. What is the importance of these italicized words? In the

beginning, the key is consistency, not necessarily every day; I suggest you might form this habit as you would if you were in an exercise program.

Additional Helps

Be realistic: Start with small amounts of time—maybe five to ten minutes, five days a week. As you continue to read through this book and apply the remaining steps, you will be able to increase the time.

Measure your objectives—possibly check your calendar after you pray each day. Keeping a prayer notebook is also a very helpful tool. This will be introduced in the next chapter, but for now, begin by asking God to lead you as you make a list of people and categories for which you can begin praying.

Set your goals with someone else if possible. The other person provides motivation, accountability, and encouragement for you.

Remember that God is excited about your effort and is looking forward to a deepening friendship!

FOUR

STEP TWO: FIND A QUIET PLACE

It was one of those perfect Thanksgiving Days—the kind you know will always be treasured in your heart. The family had flown or driven in from different parts of the country. We were to spend the holiday with my nephew and his wife, Jim and Carolyn Mead. Jim had just graduated from seminary and was serving in his first church in Portland, Oregon. Thanksgiving morning found us all sitting in church together, and a feeling of great pride swept over me when I saw my nephew stand up in the pulpit dressed in his robe, ready to bring the Thanksgiving message. I looked down at his two little boys sitting beside me. They were wearing the black pilgrim hats they had made from construction paper the day before. It seemed only yesterday that Jimmy had been a little tow-headed boy building sandcastles on the beach with his sister and my own children. Now here he was, sharing the Good News of Jesus Christ with those entrusted into his care.

After church we all went back to the manse where the delicious smells of roasting turkey and pumpkin pies greeted us. A time of happy confusion followed as the finishing touches were put on the dinner. The candles were lighted, and at last all were seated around the table. Later in the afternoon when the men were watching the football game and the ladies were visiting, I walked into one of the bedrooms and found four-year-old Dean sitting alone on the floor, holding his big black pilgrim hat on his lap. When I asked him what he was doing, he replied (with a look of utter contentment on his face), "I'm just sitting here being quiet, Aunt Hope." As I walked from the room, I thought to myself, *He has found the secret that many of us never discover in a lifetime.* In the midst of all the laughing and shouting, little Dean had found a quiet place to restore his soul. Have you found such a place?

The second step on the learning to pray ladder is: *Find a quiet place.* Jesus said this was so important that if the only quiet room in your house is a closet, then you should go in there and shut the door and pray. "But thou, when thou prayest, enter into thy closet, and when thou hast shut thy door, pray to thy Father. . . ." (Matt. 6:6 KJV).

For the past twenty-seven years, our home has been full of people; in fact, many weeks well over two hundred pass through it. Young Life meetings have been held here throughout the past nine years—small Bible studies and discussion groups, people coming for counseling, plus all the activities of three growing teenagers and their friends. Sometimes we feel our house is a motel with friends dropping in from all over the world. We enjoy it and would not want it any other way, but there are times when it is difficult to find a quiet place to pray. I can recall several occasions when the only quiet place I could find was the bathroom! I would sit on the floor, lean against the door, and pray. Maybe the only quiet place in your house is your closet. Then you're going to have to go in there, sit on the floor with all the shoes, and pray. But you *must* find a quiet place. And you will, if you really want to.

I would suggest a bright, sunny room that is cozy and filled with a sense of peace. Perhaps your bedroom is a place like that. If it isn't, you can make it into such a room. Usually our bedroom is the one place we can go and shut the door and be alone.

If your children are married and gone, perhaps you could make one of the extra bedrooms into a prayer room. When our twenty-five-year-old son, Tom, moved out on his own, we turned his room into a cozy, Early American prayer room. The first time he came home and saw his old room, he said, "Good grief—it looks like George Washington slept here!"

My daughter, Debbie, is a sophomore in college, living in a dormitory full of chattering girls. Trying to find a quiet place to pray was a real challenge for her. She found that her roommate had some classes when she didn't. This was the perfect time to go to her room, lock the door, and be alone with God in prayer. It took discipline. She could use that time to be with her friends or go to the Hub and get a Coke. But prayer has always been an important part of Debbie's life, and when you want to do something, you will find a way to do it.

Sometimes it takes your creative imagination. My friend Nancy Metz is a young mother with two "busy" children under five years of age. Trying to find a quiet place in their little house seemed almost impossible. She tried praying in her bedroom, but her children didn't like the door closed. It worried them, and they would interrupt her every few minutes. One snowy morning she turned on the television. There was a good educational program on for children, and they thoroughly enjoyed it. The following morning Nancy turned the television to the same station. She sat down with her children and explained that while they were watching the program, she would be in her bedroom, with the door open, talking to Jesus. If they needed her, they could come and get her. It seemed to solve the whole problem. She was able to have half an hour alone with God in prayer, and her children were watching a good program. One day her little boy and his neighbor friend came up to peek into the room. Nancy heard him explain to his friend as they walked away, "My mom's talking to Jesus!" How wonderful for this little boy to grow up in a home where he has seen his mother on her knees in prayer every day. Can you imagine the strength and comfort and encouragement this will be to him as he faces the problems of growing up?

When you find your quiet place, relax and unwind for a few minutes. Remind yourself that Jesus is there with you. He loves you and is looking forward to fellowship with you. He accepts you just as you are, and He cares about every tiny detail of your life. *Picture* Him there with you.

I want to share with you something that has been of great help and value to me for many years. When I kneel down to pray, I have a beautiful little room *in my mind* where I can go and meet Jesus. Actually, I guess you would call it a one-room cottage. It is set in the quiet, rolling hills of New England. There is a flowered pathway leading up to the cottage door. When I first found my little room, I spent all my spare moments for the next three weeks furnishing it in complete detail. I covered the walls with a small-patterned, blue-and-white paper. The floor is highly polished dark wood with a large oval hooked rug. Across from the curtained Dutch door is a Williamsburg Colonial fireplace where a warm fire burns cheerily. To the left of the fireplace is a pretty bay window hung with lace curtains, and a lovely antique desk sits next to the window. In the middle of the room, in front of the fireplace, is a large country-styled couch filled with one hundred percent down feathers. On either side of the fireplace are two soft, comfortable chairs upholstered in a small navy and cranberry print. Whenever I come into the room, Jesus is sitting in the chair on the right. I have an old grandfather clock on one wall, and the wall by the Dutch door is lined with a ceiling-to-floor bookcase filled with *leather-bound* books.

On the right side of the fireplace there are French doors opening out onto a small brick terrace. There is a hammock and a round table with two chairs on the terrace, and sometimes on a hot summer day the Lord and I sit out there while we talk. Near the patio is a beautiful garden with all kinds of brightly colored flowers and shrubs. The lawn is an emerald green, and there are woods of tall, stately maple and oak trees on all sides of the garden. At the end of the garden is a lovely weeping willow tree, where I often sit and talk with Jesus. Because He is there, I have no fear of intruders or ants or spiders!

My little New England cottage is a place of total beauty and tranquillity. The moment I walk through the door into my room and see Jesus sitting there, a feeling of peace and quietness fills every part of me. How easy it is to sit down in the chair opposite Him and just begin to share. No matter what the turmoil may be in my life—the loss of loved ones through death, the heartache of a child experimenting with drugs, the disappointments and hurts of daily living—all of these seem to fade into the background when I walk into my room and see Jesus.

The nice thing about my room is that it goes everywhere with me! I remember flying from the Philippines to Australia. It was an all-night flight and often bumpy. I am not the world's best flier, and when the plane starts to drop, I get panicky. I knew when we landed in Australia the next day we would be going immediately to a luncheon engagement, and I felt I needed a good night's rest. So on the bumpy plane flying over the dark ocean, I entered my beautiful little room, and there sat Jesus. He knew how tired I was and told me to lay down on the couch by the fire. He covered me with a brightly colored afghan and said to me, "Don't be afraid, Hope. I am with you. I give to you My peace. Now lie down and go to sleep." And you know, that's exactly what I did!

I would like to encourage you to fix up a comfortable room in your mind. Furnish it in *detail*—that's the secret to making it real. (I have some lovely antique pieces in my room that I could never afford to have in real life.) Make it yours. Decorate it according to your own personality, and you will find it will be a place of great peace and joy.

My sister Marilyn loves the ocean. She has made her "quiet place" a beautiful, peaceful beach scene, complete with palm trees, the sound of waves, and warm sunshine. There she walks with Jesus on the beach each day.

Maybe you like the mountains. You can build a one-room chalet high up in the Swiss Alps! The world is your limit—use the creative imagination God has given you.

This one suggestion alone can change your whole prayer life.

Oh, what an inexpressible gift is the privilege of prayer! How great His infinite love in providing us with it! My friend Sue, whose face shines with the love of Jesus, said to me recently, "If everything were taken from me but one thing, I would ask to keep prayer." Is this the way you feel?

Before closing this chapter on a quiet place, I would like to suggest three things that can help your prayer time.

First, kneel down when you pray, if possible. Obviously my schoolteacher friend, praying in the park, cannot kneel down to pray. Buy if you are praying in your bedroom, it is good to kneel. We know that positions are not important. We have talked about praying when we walk down the street, when we drive our cars, or even while we are talking to another person. But for your time of worship and intercession, try kneeling down. It is an outward sign of the inward respect you have for God. If you can't kneel, then sit up straight. This will keep you alert. By no means say nighttime "pillow prayers." You know, those are the kind you pray when you jump into bed all tired and worn out. You bury your head in your pillow and start mumbling your prayers. Before you know it, your mind has wandered on to other things, or you have fallen asleep before you finished your first sentence!

Second, pray out loud. I don't mean in a normal talking voice, but in a quiet voice or audible whisper. This will help keep your mind on what you are saying. If you are not accustomed to praying out loud in your personal prayer time, you may feel a little strange at first. I know I did when my husband first suggested I pray this way over twenty-seven years ago. But after a couple of weeks, I got used to it.

Third, write your prayer requests down on a piece of paper. Buy a small notebook and use it as a prayer notebook. Keep it by your bed. Make a page for your spouse, one for yourself, and a page for each of your children. Divide another page into family members outside the home. Have a page for the friends you promise to pray for and a page for all the other requests you want to bring before the Lord. Leave the reverse side of the page empty so you can write your answers down as God sends them.

Keeping a prayer notebook will help you pray specifically. I believe God wants us to ask Him for definite things, rather than, "God bless my family; God bless my friends; God be with my church and all the people around the world." General prayers like this can only bring general answers. Know what you are praying for. When you pray a specific prayer, you know what kind of an answer to expect. Having a prayer notebook keeps you from praying "gimmie" prayers (Lord, give me this and give me that). It keeps you aware of the needs of those around you.

One of the most important benefits from keeping a prayer notebook is that it teaches you to be thankful. When you begin to write down the answers to your prayers, you will suddenly realize how many God has answered. It's so easy to forget our answers to prayer, isn't it? Haven't you often said to yourself, "God never seems to answer my prayers"? When you feel this way, get out your prayer notebook and read over the answers God has given to you during the past month. You will be in for a pleasant surprise! You will close your notebook with a heart filled with thanksgiving, your faith will be strengthened, and you will come away praising God that He is indeed a God who loves to answer prayer!

STUDY GUIDE

1. In Matthew 6:6, Jesus tells us where to pray. What is the point of His illustration?
2. Explain briefly why this second step is so important in light of the previous question.
3. Once you have found your own quiet place, what are five good reminders you need to tell yourself?
4. How will these reminders make a difference in your prayer time with God?
5. Describe briefly the prayer room idea. What is its purpose?
6. Read Hebrews 9:1–8 and 10:19–23. Explain the biblical basis for coming into God's presence. How could you use the profound truth of this passage for your own prayer room idea?
7. How can your own prayer room idea benefit your time with God? List as many benefits as you can think of.
8. What are we really doing each time we spend quality time with God? What part of the tabernacle do we enter into?
9. Describe briefly your own quiet room or place. Be creative and specific.
10. In the last part of this chapter, the author gives three practical suggestions for your prayer time. What are

they? Give two reasons why each suggestion will help you during your prayer time.

11. Now begin your own prayer notebook. You might find it helpful to divide your prayer requests so that you pray for different ones on different days throughout the week. This prayer calendar provides variety, more opportunity for in-depth prayer, and motivation to pray each day. Here's a sample:

Monday	*Tuesday*	*Wednesday*
Myself	Friends	Neighbors
Spouse–marriage	Church	Missionaries
Family–names	Pastor	Parents

Thursday etc.
Miscellaneous needs
Areas of need in the world
Government–society

There might be certain areas for which you will pray every day—that's good. This sample prayer calendar is simply to cover the areas God is leading you to pray for during each week, so you do not feel you need to pray for every area each day. If you need further suggestions, share your prayer notebook ideas with a friend or fellow Christian. But remember, this notebook belongs to you and God, so be as creative, personal, and specific as you want to be.

FIVE

STEP THREE: SAY A PRAYER OF PROTECTION

"Good things come in small packages." This phrase can be applied to this chapter. It will be short but good! In fact, the omission of this step could be the reason why so many Christians have such a difficult time praying.

The third step on the prayer ladder is: *Say a prayer of protection* that the cares of the day will not crowd in upon you while you are praying. If the devil has not been successful in getting you to pray "tomorrow," he then switches to "Plan B," which is to do all in his power to distract you in prayer. (Read or reread the *Screwtape Letters* by C. S. Lewis.) Haven't you found that the minute you kneel down to pray the phone rings or someone comes to the door? All the things you know you have to do that day are suddenly magnified—the patches you need to sew on your son's jeans, the shirts you promised to iron, the cookies that must be baked for Girl Scouts, the exam to be studied for, etc. All these things seem to loom before you as an insurmountable mountain that must be tackled *at once!* A feeling of urgency sweeps over you. You simply do not have time to pray today—God will understand.

This is the devil at work—in fact, he never works so hard as when he sees you getting ready to pray! This is why Jesus told us to *watch* and pray. Watch for what? We are to be alert to the devil at work in our prayer time. We need to be covered with a shield of protection. Only then can we quench the fiery darts of distraction the devil is hurling at us.

Before you begin your prayer of worship and intercession, take a moment to ask God to surround you with a circle of His protection. I like to picture a circle of light surrounding me. *Nothing* can get through it while I am praying. I am going to be alone with God. I choose, by an act of my will, to shut out the cares and business of the day. I choose to empty my mind of all irritation and distractions.

Take a moment to breathe *out* all the tension and anxiety in your life.

Breathe *in* the love and peace of Jesus. Practice this breathing before you begin to pray.

Slowly breathe in God's peace and love. Picture it flooding every part of your being.

As you breathe out, imagine all the tension and anxiety leaving your body. Do this several times.

Thank God that He is at work in your life. Thank Him for making you quiet and relaxed in His presence.

When His circle of protection surrounds you, you will be able to relax and give yourself to the leading and teaching of the Holy Spirit. This is where your prayer must begin—with an openness and dependency upon Him.

"In every prayer the Triune God takes a part—the Father who hears; the Son in whose name we pray; the Spirit who prays for us and in us. How important it is we should be in right relationship to the Holy Spirit and understand His work!"[1]

As you surround yourself with a circle of God's protection, you will move your eyes away from yourself. You will focus on Jesus. Remember when He revealed Himself to the disciples in all of His splendor and glory on the Mount of Transfiguration? When it was all over, the Bible says, "When they looked up, they saw *no one except Jesus*" (Matt. 17:8, italics mine). Is this who you see when you kneel down to pray? Or are you so wrapped up with yourself that all you see are *your* problems, *your* disappointments, and *your* desires? Our goal in prayer is to see Jesus only—to be aware of His very self there with us. Then we can say with a full and joyous heart, "Father, *my* Father" (Rom. 8:15 PHILLIPS).

STUDY GUIDE

1. How important is it for you to pray prayers of protection? Can you think of two reasons?
2. Before you begin to pray this prayer, think of the picture the author suggests for you. What does she suggest you consciously choose to do before you begin to pray?
3. Describe the author's suggested breathing exercise. Why can this be important for your prayer time?
4. Each time you pray, the Persons of the Trinity are intimately involved in your prayer time. Examine the following verses and focused questions to help further understand Their involvement.

---

[1] Andrew Murray, *The Prayer Life* (Chicago: Moody Press,), p. 53.

a. What type of relationship do you have with the Person to whom you pray? What difference will your relationship make in prayer?
2 Chron. 6:4 Rom. 8:15 John 16:23
Matt. 6:6–10 Gal. 4:6

b. What do these verses tell you about the name of Christ? What do you think it means to pray in Jesus' name?
Eph. 3:11–12 John 16:24 Rom. 8:34
John 14:13–14 John 16:26–27

c. Do any of us know how to pray as we ought? In what way does the Holy Spirit help you pray?
Rom. 8:26–27 Eph. 2:18
Eph. 6:18 1 Cor. 14:16

7. From these passages, briefly summarize how each person of the Triune Godhead is involved every time we pray.
   First Person: God the Father
   Second Person: God the Son
   Third Person: God the Holy Spirit

In your prayer notebook, write your prayer requests and the date you begin praying on one side and leave the reverse side of the page blank for recording the answers and the date you received them.

SIX

STEP FOUR: WORSHIP AND MEDITATION

The fourth step on the prayer ladder is *worship and meditation.* As Christians living in an active world, we have lost the art of meditation and worship. We think if we just sit quietly and meditate upon the greatness of God that we are wasting our time. We should be *talking* to Him. Our prayers should be "productive" and "useful" and "to the point." Then we should get on with the business of the day. The thought of being quiet to worship God rarely enters our minds, and if it does, we really don't know how to go about it.

Recently, my husband and I were at the airport in London, England. The voice over the loudspeaker had just finished announcing that there would be a four-hour delay in our flight from London to Chicago. A loud groan went up from the passengers who were waiting to board the plane. Harry and I looked at each other in dismay. We had been away from home for several months and were weary from traveling. We had pictured ourselves arriving home that evening and were looking forward to spending half an hour with our friends Nancy and George Kandel, praying and thanking God for all He had taught us on our trip and for bringing us home safely. As we looked around the gloomy waiting room, we wondered what we could do during the next four hours. We had already been checked through security and could not leave the room.

It was then that a young couple in their mid-twenties sat down beside us. During the conversation that followed, we discovered that they were returning from a world-wide conference for teachers on transcendental meditation—more commonly known as TM. They were eager to share with us all they had learned. (I should say here that, as Christians, we must stay as far away from TM as possible. When we open our minds to *anything* outside of Christ, we are asking for trouble.) In TM, you are given an unknown word upon which to meditate. You are to sit quietly for at least *twenty minutes* in the morning and *twenty minutes* in the evening and just meditate. Your mind is to be blank. You are to repeat nothing except that word. "It doesn't matter what you meditate on," the young woman told me in all sincerity, "just as long as you meditate. If you're a Christian, that's OK; we'll give you a Christian word to meditate on."

As we boarded the plane a few hours later, my husband and I couldn't help thinking how different the teaching of TM is compared to the teaching found in God's Word. The Bible teaches us that the only One we are to meditate upon is God and His Word. "My soul, wait [meditate] thou *only* upon God; for my expectation is from him. He only is my rock and my salvation" (Ps. 62:5, 6 KJV).

We are instructed to meditate upon His *Word*. "Oh, the joys of those who do not follow evil men's advice. . . . But they delight in doing everything God wants them to, and day and night are always *meditating* on his laws [the Bible] and thinking about ways to follow him more closely" (Ps. 1:1, 2 LB, italics mine). "This book of the law shall not depart out of your mouth, but you shall *meditate* on it day and night, that you may be careful to do according to all that is written in it; for then you shall make your way prosperous, and then you shall have good success" (Josh. 1:8, italics mine). "Oh, how I love thy law! It is my *meditation* all the day" (Ps. 119:97, italics mine).

We are to meditate upon His *precepts* (or instructions): "I will *meditate* on thy precepts, and fix my eyes on thy ways" (Ps. 119:15, italics mine).

We are to meditate on His *mighty works*. "I will *meditate* on all thy work, and muse on thy mighty deeds" (Ps. 77:12, italics mine). "I will *meditate* on all that thou hast done" (Ps. 143:5, italics mine).

These are the things upon which we are to meditate—not on empty words, but on the great, majestic God of the universe! The One who put the stars in place, the One who loves us, the One who redeemed us!

Most of us have not been taught to worship. I know I haven't. But I am trying to learn what it means to meditate and to worship God. Two things are helping me.

First of all, I have gone through the Psalms and put a little star by all the ones filled with praise and worship. When I kneel down to pray, I open my Bible to one of the marked psalms and read it slowly. I do not know how to express the love and adoration I feel in my heart for God, but David did it so well. As I read those beautiful words expressed in his psalms, I make them mine. Through the

Holy Spirit, I offer them to God as the praise and worship of my heart.

The second thing that is teaching me to worship is reading the words of one of the old hymns of the faith. If you don't have an *old* hymnbook, get one. My friend found hers in a dusty corner of the church basement. Keep your hymnbook with your Bible on the table by your bed. After you have meditated on a psalm, read the words to one of the hymns. You will find yourself lifted to the very feet of Jesus by such words as:

Jesus! I am resting, resting
In the joy of what Thou art;
I am finding out the greatness
Of Thy loving heart.
Thou hast bid me gaze upon Thee,
And Thy beauty fills my soul,
For, by Thy transforming power,
Thou hast made me whole.
Oh, how great Thy loving kindness,
Vaster, broader than the sea,
Oh, how marvelous Thy goodness,
Lavished all on me!
Yes, I rest in Thee, Beloved,
Know what wealth of grace is Thine,
Know Thy certainty of promise
And have made it mine.

Or:

Jesus, the very thought of Thee
With sweetness fills my breast;
But sweeter far Thy face to see,
And in Thy presence rest.

No voice can sing, nor heart can frame,
Nor can the memory find
A sweeter sound than Thy blest Name,
O Saviour of mankind!
O hope of every contrite heart,
O joy of all the meek,
To those who fall, how kind Thou art!
How good to those who seek!
But what to those who find? Ah, this
Nor tongue nor pen can show:
The love of Jesus, what it is
None but His loved ones know.
Jesus, our only Joy be Thou,
As Thou our Prize wilt be;
Jesus, be Thou our Glory now,
And through eternity.

When you kneel to pray, spend a few moments in quiet worship and meditation with God. As you are quiet before him, you will find the Holy Spirit begin to work gently in your heart. He will bring to you the confidence that you are in the presence of the living God, whether you *feel* like it or not. He will fill you with a sense of peace, strength, and reverence. God's love will flow through you, warming your heart and enabling you to share your thoughts and desires with Him in complete trust.

This, in turn, produces a heart full of praise and joy, which is an important part of our worship. No other command is given to us more often in the Bible than the command to praise God continually. Think of all the things you have to praise Him for and *put them into words*. Make joy and praise an important part of your prayer of worship. I know of people who cry every time they pray! There was a time, a few years back, when every time I told God how much I loved Him, I would cry. Then I began to think, "How would Harry feel if every time I told him I loved him, I would start crying? I think he would much rather have me throw my arms around him with joy and tell him I love him." I'm sure it's the same with Jesus. He continually reminds us that He wants us to be filled with joy.

Of course there will be times of tears and pain, because we live in a lost and fallen world. Life is not one big bowl of cherries. We will face heartaches and disappointments. And the way we are going to come through them (and we *do* come through) is from the truths we learned when things were going well. This is why it is so important that we spend time with God in prayer and worship each day. A firm foundation is being laid in our lives. When we go through a dark period, we can come out victorious because our faith has been firmly grounded in Jesus Christ. Our strength and confidence are in Him.

One of my favorite verses in the Bible is: "The *joy* of the LORD is your strength" (Neh. 8:10, italics mine). What a great promise that is! When you feel weak and discouraged, stop! Begin to praise God for everything that comes to your mind. Yes, even in the midst of the problem you are going through. The Bible tells us, "Give thanks in all circumstances, *for this is God's will for you* in Christ Jesus" (1 Thess. 5:16, italics mine). We don't have to be thankful *for* everything, but we can give praise and thanksgiving *in* everything. There should be an attitude of joy and praise in our prayer life because we know He lives; we know He loves us; and we are confident that someday He will return.

When you worship the Lord with praise and thanksgiving, you will find the joy of the Lord filling your life, giving you His strength, warming you with a shower of His love. "I have told you this so that my joy may be in you and that your joy may be *complete*" (John 15:11, italics mine). Practice worshiping God with a heart filled with joyful praise. See the difference it will make.

"Then I heard again what sounded like the shouting of a huge crowd, or like the waves of a hundred oceans crashing on the shore, or like the mighty rolling of great thunder. 'Praise the Lord. For the Lord our God, the Almighty, reigns! Let us be glad and rejoice and honor him'" (Rev. 19:6, 7 LB).

STUDY GUIDE

1. Look up the definitions of "worship" and "meditation" in a dictionary and in a Bible dictionary. Compare the two definitions.
2. Have today's Christians lost the art of worship and meditation? What should be the Christian's goal of worship and meditation in prayer? Why?
3. In the first part of this chapter, the author makes an interesting comparison between transcendental meditation (a popular cult) and Christianity. Explain briefly what is involved in TM. As Christians, how does TM compare to our time of worship and meditation with the Lord?
4. What are some specific areas in which we can worship and meditate? Jot down the areas and appropriate Scripture verses. Plan specific ways you

can meditate and worship in each area. Here's an example to help you.

Ps. 62:5, 6—Meditate on God Himself. Make a list of His attributes or characteristics. Then praise Him for each and examine how He expresses these attributes to you.

5. What are two other practical suggestions the author gives to help you worship and meditate? Can you think of any others?
6. What will happen in your own life, and in your relationship with the Lord, when you begin to worship and meditate? Give several examples.
7. How will the prayer of worship and meditation help you during difficult times in your life?
8. Read the following psalms. Then jot down the specific areas in which David praises God.

   Ps. 134 Ps. 135 Ps. 138
   Ps. 145–150

Additional Helps

In your prayer notebook, write a different characteristic of God for each day of the week. Then worship and meditate on each one.

SEVEN

STEP FIVE: INNER-LISTENING

After you have worshiped the Lord in meditation and praise, spend a few moments listening to what God has to say to you. Remember, we said in chapter 1 that prayer is a conversation between two people who love and understand each other. So many of us today make our prayers into a speech to God. There is little conversation between us. We tend to do all the talking. It has been said: "For one person who exclaims, 'Speak, Lord, for thy servant heareth,' there are ten who say, 'Hear, Lord! For thy servant speaketh.'" I often find this to be my attitude in prayer. I have so many urgent requests I want to tell Him about that I don't have time to hear what He would like to say to me. I don't even give Him an opportunity to get a word in edgewise!

I think we have forgotten how to listen. We no longer know how to listen to our spouses; we scarcely hear what our children are *really* saying; and we have forgotten how to listen to each other. Is it any wonder, then, that we do not know how to listen to God? Did you ever stop and think that God has given us two ears and one tongue? Maybe He wants us to listen twice as much as we talk!

Listening is the giving of yourself to another person. It

is often the first mark of a loving, courteous Christian. Jesus spent much of His ministry on earth just listening to people. He listened to the cry of the blind man in the crowded, noisy street; He listened to the story of Mary Magdalene when she came uninvited to a dinner party; He listened to the plea of the lepers when no one else would go near them; He listened to Nicodemus who came to talk to Him late one night; and He even listened to the thief hanging next to Him when He was dying on the cross. Jesus spent His life listening to people, and He is still listening to you today. Do you take time to listen to Him?

How do we get to know someone? Isn't it by listening to them talk? If you want to know God, then you must take time to listen to what He has to say. "How do I listen to God?" is a question I am often asked. "Do you mean He is going to speak out loud to me there in my room?" No, He probably won't. But He will communicate with you. He speaks to you through thoughts He brings to your mind—through strong mental suggestions. He speaks to you through His Word, the Bible. That's why I always like to pray with my Bible open before me and also why I read my Bible *before* I pray. God often brings to my mind a passage or thought from His Word that I have just read before praying. As we quietly listen to Him, we can depend on the thoughts and words He brings to our minds because we have asked Him for His circle of protection in step three.

I believe *inner-listening* is a talent God has given to every one of His children, and it is step five on the prayer ladder. It is like all other talents—it must be developed, and this takes practice. We will not become efficient inner-listeners overnight. But like all worthwhile talents, the time put into learning will be worth it a hundred times over. I like to start my listening prayer time by saying, "Well, Lord, what do You have to say to me today?" Whenever you ask a question like that, you expect an answer, don't you? So be quiet and listen. He knows our hearts are open and receptive and that we are waiting for Him to speak to us. He will not disappoint us any more than you would disappoint your child when he says, "Mommy, talk to me!"

As you take time each day to develop this talent, you will find that you will become more open and sensitive to His inner voice. You will discover that not only does He speak to you during your special prayer time, but all during the day as well.

Don't be discouraged if you don't hear anything at first. And even after you have practiced listening for years, there will be times when you won't hear a thing. This is certainly normal.

One morning my friend Ann came to visit. We talked about prayer, and her face glowed as she told me about the many miraculous answers to prayer she had seen during the past year. It was exciting to hear what God had done in her life and in the lives of the people she had prayed for. Then a shadow crossed her face. She was quiet for a few minutes. When she looked up, she said, "It's been great, Hope, using these nine steps as a guide to my prayer life. But I have to tell you, at times I have a very hard time with inner-listening. I sit quietly and wait for God to speak, and sometimes nothing happens! I find myself getting uptight and anxious—and, yes, even angry. I find myself saying, 'Why isn't He saying something?' Does this ever happen to you?"

Of course it happens to me; it happens to everyone.

Don't get upset when you experience this. You have asked God to speak to you, and you have waited quietly for His response. If He has something to say, you may be sure He will say it; otherwise He will remain silent.

In those times of silence, learn to sit at His feet in quiet communion, sensing His love and presence there with you. I picture myself sitting in "my room" on the footstool at His feet, relaxing together for a few moments.

You don't have to be talking every minute to have a meaningful time with someone. Haven't you found this to be true when you are alone with your spouse or a good friend? Some of the nicest evenings I spend with Harry are when we turn on the stereo and listen to a great symphony. We lie on the floor by the fireplace and don't say a word to each other the whole evening. Yet we are together, and there is a depth and richness in our relationship that doesn't need any words.

In my counseling with women I have often heard them complain, "I took a ride up in the mountains the other day with my husband, and can you believe he didn't say *one word* the whole way home!" These women are angry and upset and even hurt. They fail to realize that often the best time spent with another person is in a relaxed companionship that needs no words.

Sometimes when we're insecure in our relationship with another person, we feel we must be talking all the time. I remember when Debbie went on her first date. I was sitting on her bed watching her get ready, and we were talking about all the worries and fears anyone has on a first date. As she put the finishing touches to her long brown hair, she suddenly turned to me with a look of horror and said, "But, Mom—what if we're driving along and no one is saying *anything!*" I sense this same fear in talking to people about inner-listening, and my advice is always the same: Don't worry about it. Relax and enjoy just being together with God.

Three things happen when you listen to God. *First* of all, when you ask Him to speak to you, He often brings to your mind someone who needs special prayer. It could be someone you haven't thought of in years, or someone you promised to pray for but have forgotten.

Let me emphasize here—if you say you are going to pray for someone, you'd better pray for them. We have the habit of repeating empty phrases. The words *I'll be praying for you* roll off our tongues glibly. Are you *really* going to pray for that person, or was it just the "right" thing to say at the time? When we went to Brazil as missionaries, hundreds of people promised to pray for us. When we returned five years later, very few had remained faithful in prayer. I believe God is going to hold us accountable for promising to pray for people and then not doing it.

Ask God to put a guard on your lips so you will never say you will pray for someone unless you intend to keep your promise. This is another reason why your prayer notebook can be of help. Whenever you say you will pray for someone, immediately write his or her name on a piece of paper and transfer it to your notebook when you get home.

As you take time to listen to God speak to you, He will often lay someone on your heart with a sense of deep urgency—someone who needs your prayers that very moment.

Something like this happened to me a few years ago. It was just before the Christmas holidays. I was getting ready to drive into town to buy some material to make a long skirt for Christmas. As I was combing my hair, the Lord said to me, "I want you to stop and go and pray." I said, "But Lord, You know I was going to pray at one o'clock today. This material is on sale, and it will be gone if I don't get there quickly." I continued getting ready. Again God said to me, "Go and pray." And again I gave the same excuse, "I'm going to pray at one o'clock, Lord." As I continued combing my hair, I began to feel a bit troubled. Finally God said, in an almost audible voice, "Go and pray *now,* Hope!" I dropped everything, went to my bed, and knelt down to pray. Not having any idea as to what I should pray for, I said, "Well, here I am, Lord. What do You want me to pray for?" There was a moment of silence, and then He said, "Pray for your father."

As I began to pray, I asked the Holy Spirit to guide my prayer because I didn't know how to pray. I knew my beloved father was very ill, and I found myself praying, "Oh, Lord, be with my daddy right now in a special way. May he be aware of Your loving presence surrounding him; take all fear from him, and fill him with Your peace and the confidence that You are with him." It was then that God brought to my mind the verse in Psalm 23: "Yea though I walk through the valley of the shadow of death, I will fear no evil: *for thou art with me*" (KJV, italics mine). I saw a dark valley, and on the other side, the sky was bursting with the splendor of great, billowing, golden clouds. As I looked more closely, I saw two people walking across the valley. I recognized them as Jesus and my father. Jesus was walking slightly ahead and was holding my father's hand. I do not know how long I knelt there—not too long—but a feeling of great peace filled me, and also a sense of wonder at the meaning of it all.

I did go downtown. I bought the material for my long skirt and came home. When I walked in the door, the phone was ringing. It was my sister, Marilyn, who lives in California. She said, "Hope, Daddy went to be with the Lord this morning!" As we talked and cried together on the phone, I discovered he had died at the very time I was on my knees in prayer for him. I can't tell you the comfort this was to me in the weeks ahead. I remember feeling so sad that my father had to die alone in a hospital room. But the Lord said, "No, Hope, he didn't die alone. Don't you remember? I was with him." And I would smile and say, "Oh, yes, Lord, I do remember. Thank You."

This experience is one of the most beautiful things that has ever happened to me. It showed me how aware God is of every single detail in my life. It showed me absolutely that God is a God of infinite love who understands and meets my every need. It showed me in such a tender way the truth that He does indeed walk through the valley of the shadow of death *with us*—we don't have to cross that valley alone. I shudder when I think how close I came to missing all that God longed to reveal to me that morning. And I wonder how many blessings I have missed in life by not taking time to listen.

The *second* thing that happens as you wait for Him to speak to you is that He gives you guidance on *what* to pray for and *how* to pray for it. (I will be talking more about this in step eight.) It is important that we know how to pray for a certain situation, and we need His guidance on *whom* we should pray for. I know I can't pray for everyone who asks me for prayer. And I don't believe God wants me to.

God gives each one of us our special bundle of prayers. The problem is that so few of us are faithful in caring for it. When we find a praying Christian, we breathe a sigh of relief and say, "Oh, good, here—you take some of my requests." We reach into our bundle and begin to transfer requests into the already back-breaking bundle of the praying Christian. If each of us would pray for the circle of people God has entrusted into our care, then everyone's bundle of prayer would be equal and no one would have too much.

When you are faced with a difficult decision, you need to ask God how to pray. He wants to show you His will. So many times we think God is playing games with us. We think He is trying to make it as difficult as possible for us to know His will. But our God is a God of love. He will never play hide-and-seek with His beloved children—ever! He is far more desirous of showing us His will than we are of knowing it. Do you believe that? He is waiting for you to hear Him say, "This is the way—walk ye in it," and He says this to us in many different ways.

Last Sunday night the phone rang. When I picked it up, I heard a discouraged voice say, "Hi, Mom, this is Dan. I need your prayers." Dan is in his first year at seminary and has only been there a few weeks. Before he went, he had prayed about what God wanted him to do outside of school. All the students must either work in church or do some other form of Christian service. He also had prayed that God would supply his financial needs because he didn't have much money.

I asked Dan what he wanted me to pray about. "Well," he said, "I don't know whether to work in Young Life or not. There is a high school near the seminary. A group of women have been praying for several years that God would send a leader to it. I have been asked to go." A long pause followed. Then he said with a heavy sigh, "And this real nice lady wants me to come and live with her family. She will give me free room and board. She lives just half a block from school and,"—his voice picked up here—"she has a tennis court and a swimming pool. I could save about $125 a month by moving out of the dormitory to her house."

"Well," I said, "how do you feel about it?"

"I don't know," he answered. "I think God wants me to do these things, but I'm not sure."

1. Dan had prayed for God to show him His will.
2. Dan sincerely wanted to obey that will.
3. God had opened doors for him.
4. Dan felt it was what God wanted.

As the last step, he needed to *act* on what God had revealed. If it wasn't what God wanted, then we had faith enough in His love for us to believe He would shut the door.

I think many times the devil tries to keep us from *acting* on the facts God has shown us. We are not going to get any signs in the sky or any burning bushes in our front yard! We already have far more than that. We have the Holy Spirit who lives within us! He opens all the necessary doors, but we won't sense the peace of God's will in our lives until we put our faith into action and walk though the door. On the other side of the door, we can look back and see how God was leading us all the time. But we will never know unless we *act*—unless we step through the open door. As long as we are wallowing in a sea of indecision, we are incapable of being effective for the Lord. We have made, "How do I know God's will for my life?" into an insurmountable problem, and God never intended it to be that way. As we live close to Him each day, wanting only His will for our lives and being willing to obey that will, then we can trust Him to show us the way.

Third, as you sit quietly at Jesus' feet, listening, He will bring to your mind some fault or sin, some place where you have failed Him in the last twenty-four hours. Maybe you were angry or irritable with your spouse last night for no good reason. Perhaps you didn't take time to be with your children. You were so anxious to get them stuffed into their beds so you could watch the beginning of the movie on TV. You didn't take time to read them the story you promised. You didn't take time to pray with them. Maybe you wounded a friend through gossip, or failed to write that letter to your parents when you know how much they want to hear from you. God gently but firmly goes through our past day with us and shows us where we failed. Then we need to tell Him we are sorry, which brings us to step six on the prayer ladder—confession.

STUDY GUIDE

1. Review the definition of prayer given in chapter 1. What is implied in this definition? How important is listening in prayer?
2. Look up the definition of listening in a dictionary. Compare it with the definition of listening the author gives.
3. What do you communicate to a person when you make the effort to listen attentively? List three things and then decide how each relates to your relationship with God?

4. Listening is not an easy skill, but it is so essential in your relationship to God. The author gives several helpful suggestions to get you started on this step. Answer the following questions to focus on her suggestions.
   a. What question can you ask God before you begin listening?
   b. Read John 14:21 to find what important condition you must meet to be able to hear God's voice?
   c. How did David and Abraham meet this condition?
   d. What are some ways in which God speaks to all of us today? Cite three. Which of these has God used in your own life? Think of some specific examples.
5. Will you become a good listener overnight? Explain.
6. If God doesn't speak to you right away, what should your attitude be?
7. According to the author, what are three things that will happen when you listen? List and explain briefly, then include any others you can think of.
8. When God speaks to you, what do you need to do with the information or direction He gives? Explain how this relates to knowing and doing God's will.
9. What will happen in your day-to-day Christian life when you learn to make inner-listening a real part of your time with Him?

Begin a journal section in your prayer notebook when you receive answers where you feel God is speaking directly to you and where you're learning from someone else, from Scripture, from Christian books, or from the council of other Christians. This part of your prayer notebook will help develop your skill in listening as well as provide a record of what God is teaching you.

EIGHT

STEP SIX: CONFESSION

When our daughter, Debbie, was four years old, she loved to make mud pies. I remember how she used to labor over them, making them just the right size and setting them out in the sun to dry. One morning my husband arrived home unexpectedly. Debbie was up to her elbows in "baking." When she saw her daddy, she dropped everything and ran over to him, waving her chubby arms, which were dripping with mud! I can still hear what he said to her that day. He looked down at her with love and said hastily but gently, "Go wash your hands first, honey."

Don't you think this is what Jesus has to say to us many times? We go rushing into His presence with a heart full of things to tell Him, and He has to stop us and tell us gently, "Go wash your hands first."

This is what confession is. It is coming to the fountain filled with the blood of Jesus Christ and having our sins washed away. It is being cleansed and forgiven. It is being clothed in the spotless robes of His righteousness! First John 1:9 tells us: "If we confess our sins, he is faithful and just, and will forgive us our sins and cleanse us from *all* unrighteousness" (RSV, italics mine). I like to think of this verse as my spiritual washcloth, something I must use every day.

Confession is the sixth step in prayer. There are times when you will want to put it before your prayer of worship and meditation. None of these nine steps are rigid rules that must be in a certain order or God won't hear your prayers. They are simply suggestions to help your prayer life become more effective. You can change them around or put them in any order that pleases you. You can use them as a guide when you pray for five minutes, an hour, or all day. But however you use them, confession must be a part of your daily prayer. Before you can pray effectively for others, you must first be a clean channel through whom God can work. Your heart must be clean and free from unconfessed sin.

When you come to the confession part of your prayer, pause for a moment or two and ask the Holy Spirit to go into your life with His searchlight. Let this light sweep through each corner of your life and reveal to you everything that is keeping you from becoming *all* that God created you to be.

Let David's prayer become your daily prayer. "Search me, O God, and know my heart! Try me and know my thoughts! And see if there be any wicked way in me, and lead me in the way everlasting!" (Ps. 139:23, 24). When the searchlight of the Holy Spirit stops on a certain sin, be honest enough to look at it, to acknowledge it as sin, and to confess it. Ask God to make you truly sorry—Peter was so sorry he wept. Ask God to make your heart tender and alert so you won't continue in that sin.

There is nothing as destructive as sin. A whole book could be written about that statement. Just look at the world around us and see if this isn't true. The continual wars, man's inhumanity to man, the starving millions of the world, the greed, the lust, and the hate we all read about every day in our newspapers. *Nothing* destroys more than sin. One of the most holy, sacred relationships God has ordained, the relationship between a husband and wife, has been almost totally destroyed by the sin of selfishness, uncontrolled passion, and disobedience to God. Sin destroys our fellowship with God and our relationship with others. Sin blinds us to the truth of God's Word. As we go day after day without confessing our sins, we find our spiritual eyes becoming weaker; everything becomes gray. There is no longer any black or white, any right or wrong, and finally we become totally blind spiritually. We are no longer capable of recognizing sin as sin.

A few years ago I was talking to a Christian woman. She was a Sunday school teacher and respected by all. At the time of our conversation, she was having an affair with the choir director. Both were married. As she related this story to me, she told me, in all sincerity, "But, Hope, this isn't just some cheap affair you read about. This is different—why, *our love is from God!*" The sad part is, she really believed it! She was totally blind to her sin. Eventually their sin destroyed their homes, their loved ones, and, in the end, themselves.

The wages of sin is *always* death (Rom. 6:23). This verse is addressed to Christians, not to the unsaved, as we so often use it. Make no mistake about it—as Christians, we reap exactly what we sow. "Do not be deceived: *God cannot be mocked.* A man reaps what he sows" (Gal. 6:7, italics mine). If we sow sin and destruction in our lives, this is exactly what we are going to reap.

I beg you to beseech God daily, to keep your eyes from being blinded to the sin in your life! Pray that not one thing will escape the searchlight of the Holy Spirit as it sweeps through your life. Don't permit any sin, regardless of how small or insignificant it may seem, to lodge in your life for one single day.

1. See it as sin.
2. Acknowledge it as sin.
3. Confess it as sin.

Confession is an important part of our prayer because our prayers form a channel through which God's power can pass and touch the world. If the channel is blocked by sin, our prayer becomes weakened. Sometimes the channel can become so blocked it is impossible for God's power to get through at all.

When my sons, Tom and Dan, were little, they liked to play in the ditch that ran in front of our house. It was especially fun after a rain because there would be more water in it. They would collect stones and place them, one by one, across the ditch. Finally all the water would be dammed up, and only a small, weak trickle could pass through. This is what happens when we have unconfessed sin in our lives. Our prayers get through, but the power is not there. The force is weakened by stones we have placed across the channel.

We have many stones in our lives. There are stones of hate or resentment—someone we just can't stand. There are stones of fear and worry—refusing to trust the promises of God. And there are stones of disobedience and self-will.

There is the big stone of self-pity. As Gert Bahana says, we become president of the "Poor Me Club"!

There is the stone of seeking our own "self-fulfillment," the attitude of "after me, you come first." We become totally absorbed with ourselves, with our personal happiness, and with the pursuit of finding our "self-fulfillment." In the process we often neglect our spouses, our children, and our homes. Then we wonder why our lives seem so empty.

Take a few minutes to search your life now and remove some of the stones that are blocking God's channel of love and power. Be specific when you come to the confession part of your prayer. *Name* your sins one by one. Deal with each one as God brings it to light.

It's so easy to rattle off, "Lord, please forgive all my sins," and then quickly rush on to the next part of our prayer—the part where we get to ask Him for things! There is no room for sorrow or repentance in this kind of confession. There is no time to sense the love and forgiveness that flood our hearts when we confess our sins.

Take time after confession to let Jesus wash you clean. Picture Him clothing you in the dazzling robe of His righteousness and sending you out forgiven and cleansed. Only then can you say with a full heart, "I will greatly rejoice in the Lord, my soul shall exult in my God; for he has clothed me with the garments of salvation, he has covered me with the *robe of righteousness*" (Isa. 61:10a, italics mine).

As the healing ointment of confession and forgiveness opens our blinded eyes and restores our soul, we find a desire in our heart to forgive others. After all the other stones have been removed, we sometimes see for the first time that we have an unforgiving attitude toward another person. Jesus said if we want our prayers answered, we must first forgive *anything* we are holding against another person. He didn't say it was a nice idea if we could forgive them; He said we *must!*

The degree to which we are able to forgive others is the degree to which we can be open to the love of Jesus in our lives. Do you remember who hurt you last year? I have a friend who remembers every negative thing anyone has ever said about her. For the past twenty years she has written it all down in a little book. Jesus said, "And whenever you stand praying, you *must* forgive anything that you are holding against anyone else, and your Heavenly Father will forgive you your sins" (Mark 11:25 PHILLIPS, italics mine). Don't miss out on the joy and freedom that will be yours when you can honestly forgive others.

Three wonderful things happen when we confess our sins. *First* of all, Jesus *forgives* our sins. Do you really believe that? Are you living today in the joy of being completely forgiven? I think one of the most beautiful words in any language is *forgiven.* We are pardoned from all sin and released from all guilt. The slate is washed clean!

Recently a friend tried to take her own life because she could no longer bear the guilt she was carrying around with her. When she was finally able to accept God's forgiveness, she became a new person in Christ Jesus. All things became new. A radiant smile broke through her tears, and she said, "Oh, it's gone—the guilt is gone!" Do you sense her feeling of relief! Because the sin and guilt were removed from her life through the shed blood of Jesus, for the first time she was able to forgive herself!

Have you learned what it means to forgive yourself? This seems to be one of the most difficult things for people to do. They are still remembering what God has long ago forgiven and forgotten! "There is no one harder to forgive than oneself. Nevertheless we know inside ourselves that it must be done, for remorse is a sin that rots away the very vitals of the soul. And we know well the price of a soul to God. If God and His saints in their divine foolishness put such a price upon our soul we should not let it rot."[1]

The *second* thing that happens when we confess our sins is that Jesus *comforts* and *reassures* us of His great love. Isn't this exactly what you do with your children? When they do something wrong and stand there with big tears rolling down their cheeks, crying, "I'm sorry, Mommy, I'm sorry!" you take them into your arms, tell them you forgive them, and reassure them that you still love them. This is exactly what Jesus does. Whenever you tell Him you are sorry for your sins, He tenderly puts His arms around you and says, "I know—and I forgive you. This is why I died—to take care of your sin. You are My child, and I love you."

The *third* result of confession is that Jesus encourages us *with words*. Remember the woman taken in adultery? After all her accusers had left, Jesus turned to her with love and understanding and forgave her. Then He said, "Go, and sin no more." I find those to be great words of encouragement. *Go* is an action word. It's like He was saying, "OK, you blew it. But you're sorry, and I forgive you. I love you—now get on with living. Don't wallow in this sin. It's over and done with. It's forgiven and forgotten. I have many things for you to do in your life—let's get on with living! *Go!*" Too many people miss out

---

[1]Elizabeth Goudge, *Joy of the Snow*, p. 284.

on all God has for them because they are still groveling in remorse for sin that Jesus has long since forgiven.

He is the only one who can turn forgiveness into a beautiful memory. Jesus is so *happy* to forgive us! This is why He came into the world—to take away our sin. When we confess our sins, He isn't sitting in some far-off heaven, groaning, "Oh, no—here she comes again with her sin!"

Rather, He is saying, "Good, she is bringing Me those sins. Now I can forgive her and get her back on the right path." When we confess our sins, the fellowship that had been broken by them is restored. Remember this: We can never lose our *relationship* with God, even though our *fellowship* with Him can be broken. Once we are born into His family, we are His for all time and eternity!

When you come to the confession part of your prayer, there should be anticipation and joy, even a shout of gladness or a sigh of relief. Is this the way you feel when you bring your sins before God? Do you have a feeling of great happiness because you know He will forgive you, the fellowship will be restored, and all the guilt will be removed?

What a great and loving God we have! Jesus said, "There is more joy in heaven over one sinner who repents than over ninety-nine righteous persons who do not need to repent" (Luke 15:7). Yes, there should be a feeling of sorrow and repentance for our sins, but there should also be a feeling of joyful expectancy in our prayer of confession.

Take a moment, right now, to thank Jesus Christ for providing forgiveness for all your sins through His death on the cross.

STUDY GUIDE

1. Why is confession so important? Give two reasons from this chapter.
2. Read Psalm 32:1–8, Proverbs 28:13, and Psalm 38: 1–6. What do these verses tell you about the consequences of unconfessed sin? What is the result of confession?
3. There seems to be a difference between our *relationship* with God as Christians and our *fellowship* with Him. Which is permanent and which is conditional? How is this difference seen in a father-child relationship? How does it help you understand the importance of confession?
4. How should you prepare for confession? Read Psalm 139:23, 24.
5. Confession is a two-step process. The first step deals with what is actually involved in confession from our perspective; the second is dependent on the first. Answer these questions to help gain a deeper understanding of confession.
   a. During confession, what should be your attitude toward sin?
      Matt. 4:17 2 Cor. 7:9, 10 Matt. 5:4
      James 4:8–10
   b. What does "to repent" mean?
   c. What is the nature of sin according to Romans 6:23 and Galatians 6:7–8? Does the word "death" in Romans 6:23 mean more than just physical death? Consider looking up "death" in a Bible dictionary for additional information.
   d. According to the author, "there is nothing as destructive as sin." List three ways sin destroys.

Think of examples of each in your own life as well as in our present society.

e. What three things do we need to do to confess sin?

f. What are some of the "stones" that block people's lives from God's fullness and power? Which stones do you find in your own life?

6. The second step of confession is exciting. It's really the whole purpose of confession and deals exclusively with the results. Answer these questions to help gain a better understanding.

   a. What do the following verses say about the result of confession?

      Isa. 43:25 Isa. 44:22–23 1 John 1:9
      Isa. 61:10 Phil. 3:13–14

   b. When you receive the benefits of forgiveness, why is it so important to forgive one another? Read Colossians 3:13–15; Ephesians 4:32; Matthew 6:12, 14; 18:21–35.

   c. Name three wonderful happenings when you confess your sins. Explain each in some detail.

   d. In light of the second step of confession, what should your attitude be as you approach this all-important step of prayer?

Optional Study on Confession

Psalm 51 is one of the greatest examples of confession we find in Scripture. It is David's confession to God after he has been confronted by the prophet Nathan for his sin against Bathsheba and the murder of her husband Uriah.

1. Write out this psalm of confession in your own words.

2. From your understanding of David's confession, answer the following questions:
   a. Where in David's confession does he acknowledge God's character?
   b. Which step of prayer could he be demonstrating here?
   c. When does David say he became a sinner?
   d. What does this tell you about human nature? Are we sinners because we sin or do we sin because we are sinners?
   e. Who has David sinned against?
   f. What is the result of David's confession?
   g. What does he acknowledge God will do for him?
   h. What will David be able to do when he is forgiven and cleansed?
   i. What is his new attitude?
3. Briefly explain what this psalm teaches you about confession.

You may want to include in your notebook specific areas of your life that you've given to God in confession, how you are growing in these areas, what you can do to continue growing, and also what areas you need to grow in to be able to forgive others.

NINE

STEP SEVEN: THE PRAYER OF FAITH

This is the third morning in a row I have tried to sit down and write this chapter. So far, it has amounted to nothing but piles of discarded paper and endless hours of staring at the wall. (I know every mistake in the wallpaper that was put up several years ago!) Until now, I have been writing from experiences that have proved true in my life, and I have enjoyed sharing them with you. Now I find myself at the heart of the book, and in that connection I have an unhappy experience to relate.

We have a dear son, Tom, who is twenty-five years old.[1] When he was nineteen and starting college, the drug culture was at its height in our country, and it wasn't long before he became somewhat involved in it. Last week we received a phone call from him saying he would be coming home. (He has been working in California for the past year.) How happy we were at the thought of seeing him again!

Tom arrived home a few days before I was to start writing this chapter. He brought two friends home with

[1] Stories in chapters 9 and 12 used with Tom's permission.

him. As the days passed, we learned he had become involved with a group of people who live on a river and worship nature and the gods. In their search for freedom, they have done away with most moral standards. They are critical of anyone who is not "free" like themselves. They believe Christians are bound by rules that keep them from being "themselves"; the river people are the real, honest people of the world. As my husband and I listened to him talk, our hearts became heavy.

When we went to bed last night, it was with a feeling of sadness. We had just gone through the ugly experience of Tom's "honest" friend stealing all my Christmas shopping money and four hundred dollars' worth of jewelry. It left all of us shaken, including Tom.

When my husband came down to breakfast this morning, there was a droop to his shoulders and a sad line around his lips. Just yesterday he had eaten lunch with a friend and the pastor of one of the largest Presbyterian churches in the country. When the pastor was introduced to Harry, his face lit up with surprise. He said, "Harry MacDonald! Why, you're the one who led me to the Lord twenty-nine years ago in a Young Life meeting!" As Harry told me this story over a cup of coffee, tears came to his eyes. He said, "God has used me to help so many other kids, but I can't seem to help my own son." And with that, he left for work, and I came down to write this chapter on "praying with faith"! Can you see what an ironic situation I was in? Me, writing on the prayer of faith, when I felt like throwing the whole book in the wastebasket! How could I possibly write on faith when my own faith had been shaken to the foundation? Where has God been these past five years while my husband and I have been praying our hearts out for Tom?

As I sat down to read my Bible, the phone rang. I don't answer the phone on the three days I write each week, yet I felt compelled to. It was my friend Nancy Kandel. She said, apologetically, "I know I shouldn't bother you, Hope, but I felt I had to call you." Nancy is the kind of friend you can be honest with. You know she will hold as a sacred trust anything you tell her. (I hope you have a friend like that, and I pray you are that kind of friend to others.) Because I sensed her love and know of her deep commitment to Jesus Christ, I found myself pouring my heart out to her—like a dam let loose.

When we finished our conversation, Nancy said, "Tell me, Hope, what are the promises God has given to you about Tom?" I stopped short. I had spent the last three days seeing only the outward hopelessness of his situation. I had been swallowed in a pit of black despair. I stammered a bit, and then began to tell her some of the wonderful promises God has given to me these past five years about Tom. And a strange thing happened. A warm ray of sunshine began to creep through my cold, fear-gripped heart. As I quoted more promises, the warmth of God's love and peace began to flow through my whole body. When I hung up the phone, I came back to my room and opened my Bible. I read every promise that had Tom's name written after it, with the date in the margin when God had given it to me.

After I finished reading the promises, I found a tiny seed of faith had taken root where the doubt and despair had been. I know that God indeed is the God of the universe. He is the God who moves in space and time and history. He is the God who is at work *now* in Tom's life.

He is teaching me that if I have faith, even the size of a tiny mustard seed, I can say to the mountain of despair, "Go jump in the lake!" And it will go! "Have faith in God," Jesus said. "I tell you that if anyone should say to this hill, 'Get up and throw yourself into the sea,' and without any doubt in his heart believe that what he says will happen, then it *will* happen!" (Mark 11:22, 23 PHILLIPS, italics mine). God will move the mountain *if I let Him*. But during these past three days I had allowed the mountain to become so high that I could no longer see Jesus. It had completely blocked the sunshine of God's love, and I sat alone in the dark, cold shadow of the mountain of despair.

God is the only one who can move the mountains that we all have in our lives from time to time. Mountains of heartache and despair, fear and sorrow, disappointment and hurt, the loss of loved ones and loneliness. The only way these mountains will ever be moved is through our faith. Not faith in faith, but faith in the living God, the one and only true God of the Bible.

It was when I began rehearsing before God His promises, the wonderful way He has worked in Tom's life in the past, and the way He has worked in my own life over the years, that my faith began to grow. The mountain began to disappear. On the other side, I found the quiet streams of peace, the fresh, green valley of hope, and the cool, refreshing waters of God's truth. My soul and my very life were restored.

Then I remembered that this is what the men in the Old Testament used to do when faced with a mountain. They would rehearse before God, in prayer, all the miraculous things He had done for them in the past. And before they finished praying, their fears were quenched, their faith renewed, and they were able to go out in victory! Read the story of Jehoshaphat in 2 Chronicles 20 and see how he handled a similar situation. Read the wonderful promise God gave him and claim it for your own life, as I did: "Fear not, and be not dismayed . . . *for the battle is not yours* but God's" (v. 15, italics mine).

Faith is believing *before* receiving. It is through faith that we receive Jesus Christ into our life. It is through faith that God gives us eternal life. It is through faith that we look forward to being with Him and our loved ones in heaven. Every single part of our Christian life is built upon faith, and Jesus Christ is the source and foundation of our faith. "Without faith it is impossible to please God, because anyone who comes to him must believe that he exists" (Heb. 11:6). There is no way we can ever come to God, or even believe that He exists, without faith.

What is faith? The best definition I have ever found is in Hebrews 11:1: "Now faith means putting our *full confidence* in the things we hope for, it means *being certain* of things we cannot see" (PHILLIPS, italics mine). The Living Bible says faith is "the *certainty* that what we hope for is waiting for us, even though we cannot see it up ahead."

So the seventh step on the prayer ladder is *pray with faith*. Put your faith to work—put it into action and see what happens.

Sometimes people will say to me, "I've tried prayer, but it just doesn't work." This is like saying electricity doesn't work when you turn on the lamp and nothing happens. The electricity is *always* there, waiting to be put to use, but the channel can become blocked. If you put in a new light bulb, contact is made and the power can get through to light up your room. This is often what happens in our prayer life. The power of prayer is a *law of God*. It is always at work in the world. But our unbelief can block the channel so the power cannot get through. Maybe this is what has happened in your life. Ask yourself, "How different would my prayer life be if I really believed God would hear and answer my prayers?"

We must learn to pray with faith. Jesus insisted on it over and over again. The minute we stop believing the power of prayer, the devil moves in and fills our lives with doubts, worries, and fears. Worry or unbelief is one of his most effective tools in hurting God's beloved children. You may need to say from time to time, as I do, "Lord, I believe; help my unbelief!" And He will.

Now I want to mention three ways in which God answers prayer: "yes," "wait," and "no."

First of all, there is God's "yes." This is when He says, "Yes, I have heard your prayer and am already bringing about the answer." In Isaiah 65:24 we are told, "Before they call I will answer, while they are yet speaking, I will hear."

God's *second* way to answer prayer is "wait." This answer is often the hardest to accept. We can understand a direct yes. We can even accept a direct no. But "wait"—this is where our faith is tested the most. The devil often uses God's "wait" to weaken our faith and fill us with discouragement, just as he did with me this morning. I have been praying and waiting for Tom to "find himself" for five years. I couldn't help asking God today, "How much longer, Lord?" But I am learning that when my faith is grounded on God and His promises, then I can accept His "wait." I can be assured God has heard every prayer I have ever offered for Tom and He is working to bring about the answer.

Faith is being confident that, at the right time, the answer will come. Faith is the active part of our *will* to let go and believe that God is working. It is trusting God not to delay the answer *one single moment* longer than necessary. "If it seems slow, do not despair, for these things will surely come to pass. Just be patient! They will not be overdue a single day!" (Hab. 2:3b LB).

We need to remember that often it takes time for circumstances to develop before the answers can come. There may be several other people involved in the answer. Many times God has a job to do in our own lives, preparing us to receive His answer. "Prayer is not a matter of trying to persuade God to give us what we want. Prayer is giving ourselves to God so that He can work through us what He wants."[2] We must give God time to work in our lives and in the lives of those for whom we are praying.

I have a neighbor who goes out every spring to plant seeds in her vegetable garden. Now there is simply no way she can have fresh vegetables the day after she plants the seeds. She must wait for the seeds to grow and mature before she can harvest them. And it is the same with some prayer requests. We can sow seeds of prayer, and sometimes we water them with our tears. It may seem for awhile that nothing is happening, yet we know God is at work. The seed *is* growing and developing. The one thing we can be absolutely certain of is that *there*

---

[2] Agnes Sanford, *Behold Your God* (St. Paul, MN: Macalester Park Publishing Co., 1958), p. 33.

will be a harvest! Every time we water the seed with the prayer of faith, the answer is that much closer to coming.

There will be times in God's "wait" when you may be tempted to think you are not praying in God's will. But if you have asked Him to show you *who* to pray for and *how* to pray for them, then don't let a "wait" answer shake your faith. Keep on praying for that person each day, thanking God for His power at work in that individual's life.

When we pray for an unsaved loved one or a lost sheep who has wandered from the fold, we can be confident we are praying according to His will. This kind of prayer is always God's will. I remember hearing that George Müller, a great man of faith and prayer, prayed fifty-two years for an unsaved loved one, but it wasn't until some time after he died that his loved one came to know Jesus Christ as Savior. I believe our prayers go right on living and working even after we die. I am convinced that the prayers of my parents, who are now with the Lord, are being answered today in my life.

While we are waiting for God to answer, let's ask Him to help us wait with a spirit of expectancy, almost as though we were standing on tiptoe to see what He is going to do. Let's remember that we believe in a supernatural God who loves to do miracles. It is this believing faith that allows us to wait expectantly and creatively until the answer comes—always confident that it *will* come.

The *third* way in which God answers prayers is "no." God's "no" is always said in love. He alone knows what is best for us. How many times, as loving parents, do we have to say no to our children? It isn't because we do not love them; it's because we love them so much. A teenage girl said to me one time, "I would give anything if my parents would say no to me just once!" She felt they really didn't love her or care about anything she did. She was permitted to do anything she wanted, and this is not love.

Just before we were asked to go to Brazil, we were offered a large church with a lovely manse and a regular salary. It seemed like everything we thought we wanted. It was near a seminary and a college, and this was important to my husband. We were past our mid-thirties and thought perhaps our time of working with teenagers was over. It seemed an ideal situation. We prayed about it, decided to accept the offer, and began making all kinds of exciting plans and dreaming dreams of what we would like to do in the church.

Then we got a phone call asking us to go to Brazil and start the Young Life work. It shattered us. We didn't want to go. Our boys were just ready to start high school, and it seemed all wrong. When we prayed about it, we asked God to *please* let us take that nice church. But His answer to us was "no."

We went to Brazil and learned the language. My husband built a beautiful camp on a lake for teenagers where they could come and hear the message of God's love. A foundation was laid upon which the work of Young Life is still growing in that great land. There were many heartaches and times of loneliness, but there were also times of happiness and adventure in starting something new and watching God at work. No one in our whole family would have missed going to Brazil for anything in the world. God's "no" to the church opened the door for a ministry that is now reaching out to the whole world.

I like what Maria Von Trapp said: "When God closes a door, He always opens a window!" And what a window it is! "I will open up the windows of heaven for you and pour out a blessing so great you won't have room enough to take it in!" (Mal. 3:10b LB). Learn to accept God's "no" in your life, trusting that He has something better for you.

Before you take on a prayer project, stop and ask yourself, "Do I believe Jesus will do this?" He tells us in Mark 9:23, "If thou canst believe, all things are possible. . . ." (KJV). The little catchword here is *if*. So many times before Jesus healed a sick person, He would say to him, "Do you believe I can do this?" I think most of us would agree that He can do anything. But the question is, Do I believe He *will*? There is a great difference between these two words. Praying with faith is being confident that God *will* do what you ask. If you have asked Him to show you how to pray, and you can believe He *will* do it, then this is the right-size prayer for your faith. Don't try praying for things beyond your faith, or you will get discouraged. When you see God answering your prayers, your faith begins to grow stronger, and you find you are able to take on something bigger. I would suggest you start praying for the things you believe Jesus *will* do in your life and in the lives of your loved ones. As your faith grows and matures, one day you will find yourself being able to pray the kind of prayer George Müller prayed in the following story.

An old sea captain told this story to a friend. He said, "The last time I crossed this ocean, something happened which revolutionized the whole of my Christian life. We had George Müller of Bristol on board. I had been on the bridge twenty-four hours and never left it. George Müller came to me and said, 'Captain, I have come to tell you that I must be in Quebec Saturday afternoon.' 'It is impossible,' I replied. 'Very well, if your ship cannot take me, God will find some other way. I have never broken an engagement in fifty-seven years. Let us go down into the chart room and pray.'

"I looked at the man of God and thought to myself, What lunatic asylum can that man have come from? I never heard of such a thing as this. 'Mr. Müller,' I said, 'do you know how dense this fog is?' 'No' he replied. 'My eye is not on the density of the fog, but on the living God, who controls every circumstance of my life.'

"He knelt down and prayed one of the most simple prayers, and when he had finished, I was going to pray; but he put his hand on my shoulder and told me not to pray. 'First, you do not believe He will answer. And second, *I believe He has,* and there is no need whatever for you to pray about it.'

"I looked at him, and he said, 'Captain, I have known my Lord for fifty-seven years, and there has never been a single day that I have failed to get an audience with the King. Get up, Captain, and open the door, and you will find the fog gone!' I got up, and the fog was indeed gone. On Saturday afternoon, George Müller was in Quebec for his engagement."

Can you imagine the kind of faith Müller had to tell the captain to open the door and expect the fog to be gone? This is the kind of faith God has made available to us! Isn't it worth taking the time to develop our faith and learn what it means to believe God?

Agnes Sanford, in *Let's Believe,* her delightful book for children, gives this example. She tells how you can take an empty cup and go to the kitchen faucet to get a drink. You can stand there all day, knowing the water is there, but you will never get one drop in your cup until you reach out and turn on the faucet. I like to think of believing as turning on the faucet. It's putting impetus to our prayer. We can pray for years and not see much happen. But when we learn to turn our prayers on by *believing God*, we will see what great things He can do in and through us. Then we can pray the kind of prayers George Müller prayed.

Corrie ten Boom defines faith as a:

Fantastic
Adventure
In
Trusting
Him.

This believing faith is the kind of adventure God has waiting for each of us. When we learn to pray with faith, we will find our lives taking on new dimensions. There will be a new song in our hearts and the dirty windows of doubt and disbelief will be washed sparkling clean. What a great adventure God has waiting for us in the prayer of faith! Don't miss out on it!

In the next chapter, I will share with you a simple tool that can help you pray the prayer of faith.

STUDY GUIDE

1. Why does the author begin a chapter on faith with an example of her own struggle with faith? What important lesson can you learn from her sharing?
2. What does she do to regain her faith in God? What is the result? What begins to happen to her doubt? With what is it replaced?

3. The author offers three different definitions of faith in this chapter. The first is her own; the second is the classic definition of faith in Hebrews 11:1; and the final one is Corrie ten Boom's definition. Examine each carefully, noting how all three help to expound your own understanding of faith. (For additional reading about Corrie ten Boom's story of faith, see *The Hiding Place*.)
4. What are three ways God answers prayers? Explain each, especially noting how faith is involved.
5. Should you begin praying big prayers of faith? Explain.
6. What should you ask yourself before you pray the prayer of faith?

From her study of Scripture, the author shares several principles you can use to grow in faith. Read the following passages carefully to discover four major principles for growing faith.

Principle #1: Colossians 2:6–7 and Romans 5:6–11. Note that Colossians gives the principle; Romans 5 gives the argument to support the principle.

a. How did you first receive Christ as Lord (Rom. 3:27, 28)? What did you first believe? What is the source and foundation of your faith? What is the result of strengthened faith?
b. In Romans 5:6–11 four words describe your state prior to Christ's death. What are they? What is the greatest demonstration of Christ's love and faithfulness for you?

c. Now that you have accepted Christ, how are you described according to verses 9 and 10?

d. Paul uses the comparative phrases, "how much more," twice in verses 9 and 10. What is he comparing? How does this comparison give you reasons for increased faith?

e. According to verse 11, what happens to you when you realize this great truth in your life?

Principle #2: For a summary statement of this principle and supporting argument, read Romans 8:31–32.

a. Examine Hebrews 12:1–3 to discover the principle. How does it relate to the statement, "Our faith is only as good as the object in which it is placed"?

b. In 1 Samuel 17:1–51, where did the Israelites and Saul place their faith? Why were they so afraid? Where did David focus his faith? What was he able to do? What are some of the giants in your own life?

c. Read again the story of George Müller's prayer of faith at the end of this chapter. How does it relate to this principle?

Principle #3: Read Deuteronomy 5:15; 6:11–12; 8:2; Psalm 106:7, 13; Psalm 105:1–5.

a. What is the principle from these verses? What will be the result of practicing this principle according to 1 Chronicles 16:34–35; Psalm 106:1–2?

b. How does this principle underline the importance of your keeping a prayer notebook?

Principle #4: Read Romans 4:18–23.

a. What was the key to Abraham's unwavering faith in spite of the facts? What were three specific results of his faith (Rom. 4:20–21)?

b. How does this principle relate to the author's renewed faith concerning her son in the beginning of this chapter?

Conclusions

How can each of these principles be applied specifically to your own prayer of faith?

Establishing and keeping personal goals are keys to living the Christian life. Consider adding this step of faith to your prayer notebook. Pray for and plan your goals and then divide them into three or four categories. Here's a sample:

Spiritual Goals

1. 15 minutes of prayer, 4 days a week
2. 15 minutes of Bible study, 4 days a week
3. 1 verse memorized each week

Family Goals

1. Plan something special for you and your spouse to do each week.
2. Pray and share together weekly.
3. Plan a regular time to do something fun with the kids, as well as pray together each night.

Physical/Vocational Goals

These goals are personal, to be set after seeking God's wisdom in prayer. Perhaps you will want to share them with another person for encouragement and accountability.

Additional Study for Chapter 9

The prayer of faith is used especially for intercessory prayer. This is an optional study in this vital ministry of prayer.

1. Read the following verses carefully and list the specific areas of needs Paul prays for concerning his friends.

   2 Cor. 13:7–9
   Eph. 1:15–19
   Eph. 3:14–21
   Phil. 1:3–6; 1:9–14
   1 Thess. 1:2–3; 2:13; 5:13–16
   Philem. 1:4–7

   a. How do Paul's prayers differ from yours?
   b. What are the most important areas you can pray for concerning your friends? Explain.

TEN

STEP EIGHT: BELIEVING PRAYER AS ANSWERED

One beautiful autumn day my husband, our son Dan, and I went up in the mountains to cut our winter supply of wood. We each had a special job assigned to us. Harry was to saw all the dead logs that were lying on the ground. Dan's job was to split the logs, and I was to stack them in the truck. The problem was that we didn't have the proper tools for Dan to split the logs. All we had was an old broken ax and a small hammer. If you know anything about log-splitting, you know you need to have a wedge and a strong hammer or mallet. Dan must have said at least one hundred times that day, "If only I had the right tools, I could split these logs twice as fast!"

It's important that we have the right tools if we want to do a good job. Well, I have a little tool I would like to pass on to you. It has changed my whole prayer life. I am confident that if you use it, yours will be changed too. This valuable tool is also step eight on the prayer ladder. It is: *Picture the prayer as already answered.* Use the creative imagination God has given you. Construct, in detail, a picture of the prayer as answered. This only takes a few seconds to do, but, oh, the power it adds to your prayer of faith!

Now, please note that I am not talking about "creative imagery" in this chapter. Creative imagery is part of the New Age teaching, which says that we can create with our imagination. This is a dangerous heresy that is rapidly becoming popular throughout the world. A heresy, as you know, is always a distortion of the Truth. There is just enough truth in it to be acceptable; enough error in it to lead us astray from God's Truth.

Let me give you an example of what I mean. When we returned from Brazil, our daughter, Debbie, was fourteen years old. She had been away from America for six years and found it most difficult to adjust to the American way of life. In Brazil, she was riding bikes and climbing trees. Here in her junior high school, the girls were dating and smoking, and many were experimenting with drugs. She used to come home from school every day and cry. She wanted to go back to the happy, carefree days in Brazil, the days of climbing trees and laughter.

It wasn't long before her insecurity began to manifest itself in the form of fear. She was afraid to go to bed at night and afraid to stay in the house alone. You don't hire a baby-sitter for a fourteen-year-old, so I stayed home with her.

Ever since Debbie was a little girl, we have had a lovely bedtime custom. We would pray together and then have a visiting or sharing time. We continued this until she left for college, and it will always be one of my happiest memories. However, during this period of fear, I would have to look under the bed and in the closet every night before leaving her room. Now if you *really* think someone is under the bed or in the closet, it can be extremely frightening!

It was after coming home from a Young Life conference

that I began to think about praying for Debbie's fear—using the picture prayers we had learned about. I had never prayed this way before, and I was a bit apprehensive as I sat on her bed that night. I remember saying to her, "Debbie, it isn't God's will that you should be filled with this fear." And I quoted the verse in 2 Timothy 1:7: "God hath not given us the spirit of fear; but of power, and of love, and of a sound mind" (KJV). I told her, "We're going to pray that He will take this fear away from you." Then I began to pray a simple prayer. "Lord, we know this fear is not from You. We know You want to take it away from Debbie right now, and we thank You that You are doing this." I paused a minute and then went on. "And, Lord, I see Debbie with the fear completely gone. She is able to go to sleep at night without looking under her bed or in the closet. I see her with a look of peace on her face. I see her sleeping a restful sleep and waking in the morning refreshed and free from all fear. Thank You that You are now at work bringing this about."

After praying this way for two nights, the fear was gone! Not only that, but Debbie was no longer afraid to stay in the house alone. I remember the first night we left her. I was a bit anxious all evening, and my husband and I hurried home after the meeting. When we walked in the door, she greeted us with a happy smile and said, "Hi! How come you came home so early?"

That was my first experience praying "I see" prayers. I was so excited about the miracle that had happened with just this one little prayer that I could hardly wait to begin praying this way for everything. (I'll be sharing some of those prayers with you in chapter 12.)

Jesus said in Mark 11:24, "That is why I tell you, whatever you pray about and ask for, *believe that you have [already] received it* and it will be yours" (PHILLIPS, italics mine). Read that again and think about what you are reading! It will revolutionize your whole prayer life. Remember, *Jesus said it*—not me!

This promise is just as true as the ones we stake our eternal life on. Jesus said, "Believe in the Lord Jesus, and you will be saved" (Act 16:31). We believe, and we are saved. Jesus also said, "If you believe, you will receive whatever you ask for in prayer" (Matt. 21:22). Jesus said, "For God so loved the world that he gave his one and only Son, that whoever believes in him shall not perish but have everlasting life" (John 3:16). Jesus also said, "I tell you the truth, anyone who has faith in me will do what I have been doing" (John 14:12).

We cannot pick and choose which verses we want to believe. We cannot say, "I believe this verse, but I won't believe that one." God hasn't left it up to us to decide which ones we want to believe and which ones we don't. Either *all* of the things Jesus said are true or none of them are. C. S. Lewis said that Jesus Christ is either the world's greatest liar and deceiver, or He is who He says He is: God Himself, the way, the truth, and the life!

The problem is that when we read the astounding promises Jesus has given to us about prayer, we try to rationalize them. We think we must qualify these promises to fit our finite understanding. We wrap our intellectual robes around us, clear our voices, and say, "Well, you see, what He *really* means is . . . ," and off we go into some logical explanation of what we think He meant. We have to water down His Word to fit our weak, quivering faith. We do away with all the simple, direct promises He has given us because we don't see them happening in our lives. Therefore, we argue, they must have been meant for a different time in history. How many times I heard while growing up, "The age of miracles is over, Hope. This is a new dispensation." And with those two sentences, all thoughts of a supernatural God who *loves* to do miracles were swept away.

Listen! "Jesus Christ is the same yesterday and today and forever" (Heb. 13:8). Do you believe that? If you do, then you must believe when He says, "Whatever you *pray* about and *ask* for, *believe* that you have [already] received it and it will be yours."

1. We must pray.
2. We must ask.
3. We must believe we have received the answer.

Most of us are pretty good about the first two. We do pray and ask Him for things. But how many of us believe we have received the answer? Do we believe the words of the old hymn?

Thou art coming to a King,
Large petitions with thee bring;
For his grace and power are such,
None can ever ask too much!

Learning to believe God is putting faith into action. Making a picture of the prayer as already answered is teaching me *how* to believe. It is simply a *tool* that is helping me learn to believe. It is something I can understand—something I can put "handles" on. When I pray for someone now, instead of rushing on to the next request, I take a few seconds to make a picture of the result. I add a few touches of detail to the picture, and I thank God His power is now at work bringing this about *according to His will*. I have found this is the best way I know of to exercise my faith and teach me *how* to believe.

The day may come in my prayer life when I no longer need to make a mental picture of the prayer as answered. I will be able to go directly from the prayer for faith to the prayer for thanksgiving. But until that day comes, I will not part with this tool God has given to me.

There are three important guidelines I want to mention in connection with the "I see" prayer. *First* of all, if you are going to pray effective "I see" prayers, you must pray according to God's will. There is no other way. Your prayer must conform to His will and be for His honor and glory. This is why the prayer for guidance is vital. You must first ask Him to show you how to pray. Listen for His answer (we talked about this in the chapter on inner-listening) and then accept His will. The prayer of guidance and the prayer of faith are separate. You cannot combine them. If you try to, you will rob your prayer of its power. Before you pray for anyone or anything, you must first say, "Lord, show me how to pray for this situation." And don't pray until He shows you how.

Second, never use the word *if* in your prayer of faith. Don't add that faith-weakening phrase most Christians tack onto the end of their prayer—"if it be Thy will." *If* is a negative word that always brings about negative results. It completely waters down the prayer of faith. It is a word full of doubt and uncertainty. It's like you are making an escape for yourself and an apologetic excuse for God. Instead, use the phrase "according to Thy will." This is a positive, faith-building phrase that is grounded on the promises of God and His truth. He has already shown you how to pray; now go ahead, with faith, and pray *according* to His will.

Third, when we pray and make a mental picture of the prayer as answered, we must not make a picture of *how* God is supposed to work. We do not give Him a blueprint, saying, "Now, Lord, this is my request, and this is how I want You to work it out." We leave the "how" completely up to Him and His love and wisdom. We see the prayer as answered, but we do not see the "how," the details.

I remember a friend of mine was praying for her husband to commit his life to Christ. She had asked several people to pray for him as well. A few months ago, I met her in the supermarket. As soon as she saw me, she started crying. I thought some tragedy had happened to her and asked her what was wrong. "Oh," she sobbed, "my husband became a Christian a few weeks ago!" "Well," I said, "Praise the Lord! What are you crying about?" "But you don't understand. I was sure God would make him a Baptist, and he's still a Catholic!" You see, she had handed God a blueprint with the request for her husband's salvation. It said: "Make him a Christian; make him a Baptist; make him be immersed; and make him a good Christian just like me!" But we can't do that with God.

If you are praying for the salvation of a loved one, bring him before the Lord each day. Take a few moments to picture how he is going to look when he knows Jesus. You might picture him with a look of peace on his face. You might picture him shouting for joy. You might see him sitting and reading his Bible. Or you may see him as I picture Tom—standing on a hilltop, arms outstretched, with the chains that bound him lying broken at his feet. Whatever picture comes to your mind, hold it up before

God to be molded into His will and then thank Him that He is at work now ministering to your loved one.

Two years ago I was speaking about prayer at a women's retreat. After the morning meeting, a lady came up to me with an agitated look on her face. She said, "Well, Hope, I think you're all wrong about God answering prayer. I've been praying for my husband for the past twenty-three years, and he is still the same old, irritable, ugly man. He'll never change. I know it!" I asked her if she loved her husband. She replied, with a heavy sigh, "Yes, I suppose I do." I asked her to tell me one kind thing she had done for him in the past week. She had to think about that for a long time. Finally she said, "Well, I fixed his dinner every night. That was kind wasn't it?" I said, "I don't know if it was or not. Did you serve it to him with an attitude of love and kindness?"

After talking for awhile, I told her I thought she was praying for the wrong thing. Not that it was wrong for her husband to come to Jesus, but maybe she needed to start at the beginning—with herself. I asked her to pray that God would help her do one kind thing for her husband every day for the next week. We took a moment to picture her doing something kind for him. Then she needed to ask for a tender heart. She needed to ask God to forgive her for the self-righteous attitude that tainted every area of her life. We pictured in our minds how her face would look when the hard, bitter lines of self-righteousness were removed. I asked her to memorize Ephesians 4:32 and make it her verse for the next few months: "Be kind to one another, tenderhearted, forgiving one another, as God in Christ forgave you" (RSV). After praying for a kind, tender heart, I wanted her to ask God to put a real love in her heart for her husband. We pictured her with a loving look on her face. She was to look for little things she could do to make him happy. I told her what Mrs. Billy Graham says: "*Your* job is to make your husband happy. *God's* job is to make him good!" Think about that.

I didn't hear from the woman again until recently when I received a thank-you note from her. Because she really did love the Lord and had a sincere desire for her husband to know Him, she had been willing to follow through on what we talked about that day. She is becoming a kind person, and God has given her a real love and understanding for her husband. And wonder of wonders—her husband has given his life to Christ!

You see, she had been praying twenty-three years for her husband's salvation, never expecting anything to happen, and nothing ever did. It was only when she began praying a step at a time, picturing each prayer as answered and acting upon that picture, that God was able to work in her life and in the life of her husband.

Go through your prayer list and see if you need to change some of your requests. Maybe you are praying for the big result and jumping over all of the smaller important steps that could bring about the answer. You see, the prayer of faith is a miracle-working prayer. Don't waste God's time and yours if you are not going to believe Him. Picturing the prayer as answered is a simple way to teach you how to believe.

Now I want to warn you about one thing. When you begin to pray this way, the devil will bring all kinds of doubts and questions to your mind. He doesn't want you to pray the prayer of faith. He would much rather have all Christians continue praying their little weak, watered-down "if" prayers. The devil's greatest task has always been to deceive, and he has been deceiving Christians in their prayer lives for centuries. When you begin to picture the prayer as answered, he is going to come to you and say with a sneer, "You don't think that just because you are making this picture your prayer is going to be answered, do you?" Then you tell him no. *The picture has nothing to do with your prayer being answered.* It is simply a tool you are using to teach yourself to believe in God. The importance of faith is in its object, and the object of our faith is the Lord Jesus Christ. Our faith is never in a picture, or in a tool, rather our faith must always remain anchored in the living God.

Other well-meaning Christians may warn you against praying the prayer of faith because it sounds too much like the power of positive thinking. For some unknown reason, the phrase "the power of positive thinking" has become like a red flag in some Christian circles. Yet, Jesus Christ Himself was the greatest teacher of the power of positive thinking! I challenge you to read the Gospels again and see how often He used the power of positive thinking. Wouldn't it be refreshing if all Christians could put this faith, this God-given power of positive thinking, into their prayer lives?

It's true that we, as Christians, must be aware of the danger of the New Age teaching, but neither can we permit these Eastern religions to rob us of our right to pray the prayer of faith and to picture the prayer as answered according to God's perfect will, built upon the promise of God's Word. Remember why you are able to pray the prayer of faith and who told you to do so.

Many years ago, our family adopted a nine-year-old Korean boy through World Vision. We were not able to bring him to the States, but we sent a monthly check to cover his expenses in the orphanage. We enjoyed writing to him and receiving his translated answers back to us. It was a family project to go Christmas shopping for him; each package was wrapped with love and sent off with a prayer that our son would know we loved him very much.

When he was sixteen years old, the orphanage found a job for him, and we received our last letter. It was a dear letter thanking us for our love and prayers during those years. Because it was impossible for the orphanage to keep in touch with the ones who were old enough to leave, and because our son did not know any English, there was no way we could keep in touch with him.

Four years ago, my husband and I were going to Korea to visit Mr. Kim, Jong Dal. Kim is the director of Young Life in Korea and a dedicated man of God. A month before we left, I sent him the last letter we had received from our son. I asked Kim if he could try to find him, realizing it was a nearly impossible task, as there are millions of people in South Korea, and we had no idea where he was.

But we have a great God, don't we? He knows *exactly* where each one of His children is every moment of the day! Therefore, we began to pray that God would help Kim find Myung Woo, our son. We pictured ourselves seeing him for the first time and throwing our arms around him with joy. And we thanked God that He was working to bring this about. Before leaving on our trip, I went downtown and bought him a watch and a few other little presents.

When we stepped off the plane in Korea, Kim and his wife met us with happy smiles. He told us, "I have found your son. You will meet him tomorrow!"

You can imagine what a happy meeting that was! We walked into a small room, and there sat a handsome young man of twenty-two years. He was wearing a suit and tie and was looking every bit as nervous as we were feeling. We walked over to him, and Kim said, "I would like to present to you your son, Lee, Myung Woo." And it was just as we had pictured in our prayers—our arms were wrapped tightly round him and tears of joy ran down our faces. We didn't even need our interpreter, because Myung Woo had learned English. "Just in case God would ever let me meet you here on earth," he told us.

I wish I could tell you about our experiences since that time. Maybe I'll have to save them for another book! Myung Woo is a dear, dedicated Christian who loves Jesus Christ and longs to share Him with others. When he finishes his service in the Korean army, he will come over for a visit and perhaps attend seminary with his brother Dan.

The whole story is a miracle of God's love. It is one of the beautiful surprises God delights in giving us.

What happy surprise are you believing God for today? Or do you believe He is a stern God who sparingly doles out a few of our basic needs after we plead for them with tears? If you are living your Christian life that way (and thousands of Christians are), then you have let the devil deceive you again. The God of the Bible takes great pleasure in showering us with things we will enjoy. He loves to give us happy surprises! He is our Father—He is our friend—and He dearly loves us. "Be delighted with the Lord. Then he will give you all your heart's desires. Commit everything you do to the Lord. Trust him to help you and he will" (Ps. 37:4, 5 LB). Or take this promise in

Psalm 84:11: "No good thing will he withhold from those who walk along his paths" (LB). Are you walking along His path today? If you are, this promise is for you. Or are these some of the promises you have chosen not to believe because they don't fit into your intellectual thought pattern?

If you have a hard time believing that God is a God of happy surprises, then I suggest you make a prayer page in your notebook and title it "God's Surprises." Jot down two or three desires of your heart and pray about them. See what will happen!

When we returned from Brazil, my one desire was to have a fireplace. We spent five cold winters in Brazil hovering around a tiny kerosene heater. Our only fireplace was the candle in the middle of the table. I prayed, "Oh, Lord, I don't care what kind of house we have in the States, just as long as it has a fireplace, *please*." And do you know what? We have a house with *two* fireplaces!

What kind of "I see" prayers are you praying today? Are they prayers of faith and expectancy? Let me challenge you to pray this kind of prayer for just one month. It only takes a few moments to form a picture in your mind. It would probably add a total of three extra minutes to your prayer time each day. That's not much in exchange for the miracles you will see happening in your life.

I wish I could come and visit each one of you after your month of praying the prayer of faith. I would love to sit down and have a cup of tea with you and hear all the things God has done in your life and all He has taught you.

Expecting God to answer our prayer of faith is the heritage of every praying Christian.

STUDY GUIDE

1. What is the purpose of this eighth step?
2. How will using this simple step increase your prayer of faith and make it more real?
3. In Mark 11:24, we are given the promise that is the basis for this eighth step of prayer. Instead of believing this promise, what do we so often do? Why?
4. Read again Mark 11:24; what must we do (3 things)?
5. Explain briefly the three parts of this eighth step. How do these help you exercise your faith and teach you how to believe?
6. What are three important guidelines the author discusses in connection with the "I see" prayer? Explain each briefly and tell why each is important.
7. The first guideline is possibly the most essential. How can you learn to pray according to God's will (review chapter 5)?
8. In this chapter, the author mentions one important way to learn how to pray according to God's will. Read John 15:7. How does this verse shed even more light on learning how to pray this way?
10. Why is it important to learn to pray "a step at a time?" Praying in this way depends on your understanding (or picture) of God. Why?
11. What are a couple of doubts the Devil might use to keep you from praying "a step at a time?" How should you respond?

Make a section in your prayer notebook devoted completely to answered prayers. As you watch this section grow and develop throughout the year, it will become a tremendous faith builder every time you rehearse God's continual working in your life. This will prepare you for the final step of prayer.

ELEVEN

STEP NINE: TIME OF THANKSGIVING

When Tom and Dan were very young, I overheard them praying with their dad one night. All three of them were kneeling by the bed, and Tommy was closing the prayer time. He must have spent at least five minutes thanking Jesus for everything he could think of. He covered all the family and relatives, near and far. He thanked the Lord for every friend he had in school (by name). He thanked God for all the flowers and trees, sunshine and rain, moon and stars, and everything else in nature. After thanking Him for all the people around the world, he paused, turned to Harry, and said, "What should I say now, Dad?" And before Dad could answer, his brother replied, with a spurt of inspiration, "How about Amen!"

I smiled as I walked away from the room, but I have thought a lot about that since. This is the way we should end our prayers—with a heart full of thanksgiving to God for all He has done for us and with a hearty Amen, which means "so be it!"

In the last chapter, we learned that when we pray the prayer of faith, we always stop right then and thank God that His power is at work in that person's life. Then we go on to the next request. This way, the prayer of faith is combined with the prayer of thanksgiving.

Here is the pattern to follow in praying the prayer of faith:

1. Ask guidance on how to pray.
2. Make your request.
3. Make a picture of the prayer as answered.
4. Thank God that He is working to bring the answer about.

But we must also close our prayer with a special *time of thanksgiving*, for this is the ninth step on our prayer ladder. This teaches us to develop a thankful heart. As a result, we find the joy of the Lord filling every part of our lives and running over to those around us. Everyone we come in contact with during the day should be able to tell that we are a thankful person. It should be the characteristic of our Christian life.

Exactly what are you thankful for? Take a few moments to tell Him. Be specific when you come to this part of your prayer. Don't lump it all into one sentence and say "Lord, thank You for everything."

Take time to thank Him for His great love for you.

Thank Him for the gift of salvation and eternal life.

Thank Him for His continual presence in your life.

Thank Him for the Bible and for all He teaches you about Himself through it.

Thank Him for the great privilege of prayer. (How could we ever live without it?)

Thank Him for putting a desire in your heart to pray and to learn how to pray more effectively.

Thank Him for the church and the fellowship you have with other Christians.

Thank Him for the work He has given you to do. (Have you ever thought how empty life would be without it?)

Thank Him for the health and strength that enable you to work.

Thank Him for your loved ones and for Christian parents (if you are fortunate enough to have them).

Thank Him that you can be a Christian parent to your children.

Thank Him that you have eyes with which to see and ears with which to hear.

Be thankful for your home—that you have a bed with sheets to sleep between, and that you can take a hot shower. There are millions of people in the world who have never slept in a bed or had a hot bath!

Be thankful you had something to eat today—millions did not.

Oh, there are so many, many things to thank and praise God for. *Put them into words.*

When you close your prayer with thanksgiving, it causes you to get up from your knees with a positive, grateful heart. You will find yourself with a joyful spirit of anticipation and expectancy for all God has planned for you that day.

Every prayer should be closed in the name of Jesus. It is only in His dear name that we make our prayer and receive the answer.

"Always be joyful. Always keep on praying. No matter what happens, always be thankful, *for this is God's will for you* who belong to Christ Jesus" (1 Thess. 5:16–18 LB, italics mine).

STUDY GUIDE

1. What is the pattern to follow in praying the prayer of faith? What does each step affirm in this pattern?

2. What are several specific results of this final step of prayer? Why are these results so important in your own life and for those around you?
3. Recall the specific "Thank You's" for which we can all be thankful. Why is it important to be specific when you thank God, both from your own perspective, as well as from God's? How is the importance of being specific in our time of thanksgiving with God illustrated in our relationships to those with whom we are especially close?
4. Take a minute to list several specific things for which you can be thankful.
5. If you close your prayer with a specific time of thanksgiving, how will your attitude toward each day change?

Additional Helps:

Consider including one specific section of your prayer notebook for thanksgiving; possibly set aside one day of prayer a week specifically for thanksgiving.

TWELVE

IDEAS AND EXAMPLES FOR SPECIFIC SITUATIONS

In closing this book on prayer, I want to give a few suggestions and examples of how to pray in specific situations. I will not try to cover them all, because that would mean writing another book, but I will mention the ones I am asked about most often.

Praying for the sick. There are several ways in which we can pray for those who are ill, depending upon the circumstances.

A few years ago, my mother was dying of hardening of the arteries. She had always been an active woman. When I was growing up, she used to go with my father to the missions and jails, where she played the piano for the song service, and my father would bring the message. He was a businessman who was also a lay-preacher. Our home was always open to visiting missionaries, who would come and stay with us for a time of rest. My mother worked with Child Evangelism for years and always taught a Sunday school class. She could clean the house, go shopping downtown, and prepare a lovely dinner party for twenty-four people all in a single day! So when she had to spend the last year of her life in bed, you can imagine how difficult it was for her!

I remember my sister, Marilyn, wrote to me a few months after my mother had been confined to the hospital. Because of the nature of her disease, she was becoming forgetful and unkind to the ones she loved. She and my father had been hand-holding sweethearts for forty-seven years, and now she was saying things to hurt him. He would often leave the hospital room in tears.

We knew this was not God's will for my mother to end her life in a manner that was so completely contrary to the way she had lived. And so we began to pray that God would take the unkindness away from her. We pictured it leaving her body. We prayed that the Holy Spirit would fill her with His peace and quietness and love. We pictured the peace of God starting down at her toes, going through her whole body, and touching every part of her. We pictured her bed surrounded with a circle of God's love, and we pictured her with a look of peace on her face. We thanked God that He was at work bringing this about.

Within two weeks, my sister wrote to me and said, "Mother is a completely different person. All the hate and meanness have left her, and she has a look of such peace on her face that the nurses come from all over just to look at her!"

I remember that during my last visit to see mother, just before she went home to be with the Lord, the head nurse told me, "Your mother has been our favorite patient. She is always so kind and appreciative of everything we do for her."

And I believe the forgetfulness mother went through that last year, which was so hard for the family to take, was God's dear way of enabling this active, Christian woman to go through a year of lying in bed, day after day.

I want to suggest one thing for any of you who may have a loved one in a hospital or nursing home for an extended period of time. My sister and father visited my mother two times a day. Now if you have been through this experience, you know how difficult it is to think of things to say, especially when the person's mind has become so forgetful. You want to be with your loved one, and they want and need you there, but it only takes so long to ask them how they are and to tell them what you had for lunch or dinner! It's hard to stand beside the bed and wonder what to say next. And yet you don't want to leave them after a mere fifteen-minute visit. This can be a sad and frustrating experience for you to have to repeat day after day, month after month.

When my sister told me this in a letter, I prayed and asked God what we should do. He gave me this idea: "Sing hymns with her and read to her from the Bible and other daily devotional books she enjoys." I wrote and suggested this to Marilyn. I added that I knew at first she would feel embarrassed and even silly singing to my mother in the hospital ward, but that she should go ahead and do it anyway. She should try to think of the joy it would bring our mother. (Of course, it was much easier for me to write such a suggestion from Colorado Springs, knowing I wouldn't have to carry it out because I didn't live in California!)

My dear, brave sister took one of her hymnbooks and my mother's Bible to the hospital the next day. She started out by singing five or six hymns with her and then read some of the favorite passages my mother had underlined in her Bible. And my mother, whose memory was almost completely gone, would sing along with her in a perfect alto voice—never missing a word in *any* of the verses! Talk about a change! You see, her *spirit* was being fed and refreshed and renewed each day. The love of Jesus was ministering to her soul. Her mind may have long since gone, and her body wasted away, but her spirit was alive with the love and peace of Jesus. And my sister kept up that faithful ministry for one whole year! The nurses loved to see her coming because they knew the sound of music would soon be floating down the halls and into the rooms of the other patients, bringing joy and peace to them all.

A few days before my mother died, I went to California to be with her. The last day before she slipped into unconsciousness, my sister and I were sitting by her bed with the hymnbook. The three of us sang together for over an hour, my mother never missing a word or a note.

In my mother's case, we did not feel led to pray for healing. She was old and ready to go home to meet the Lord she loved and served. So we prayed instead for God's love and peace to fill her and minister to her spirit. And it did.

Praying for complete healing. I attended a luncheon recently with a few close Christian friends. One of them, Judy[1], had had a bleeding ulcer for several years. When she walked into the living room that day, she said, "I hope you all don't mind if I'm rather quiet today. My ulcer is really hurting me."

Judy felt her ulcer was a punishment for the kind of life she had lived before committing herself to Jesus Christ. (It wasn't a punishment, only the natural result.) She had lived in a wealthy suburb of Chicago on the

---

[1] Judy's story used with her permission.

North Shore with her husband and children. Their life was lived from one weekend party to the next, each hostess trying to outdo the other with elegant surroundings and gourmet food. One night, at a luxurious party given in her lovely home, Judy looked around at all that was going on—friends flirting with other people's husbands and wives; gossiping and sarcasm mingling in the air with the heavy smoke fumes; people drinking and getting drunk. She wondered, "What am I doing here? Is this all there is to life? One party after another? No purpose, no meaning?"

She walked out of her home that night, leaving the party going in full swing. It was mid-winter and five degrees below zero, but she didn't bother to take a coat—she didn't need it for what she had in mind. She drove out to a cliff overlooking Lake Michigan and, with the motor still running, was planning to drive the car over the cliff and end her life. However, in the fleeting moment before she prepared to send the car plunging into the dark water below, she cried out, "Oh, God—if You are—help me! God, please help me!"

Instantly, in a split second of time, *the God of the universe* heard that cry and filled the car with His presence. Judy said it was as though liquid love filled every part of her, from her head to her toes, and a feeling of total peace came over her. She knew it was God! She saw herself as a lost lamb being held in the crook of the Shepherd's arm, and this picture has never left her.

She turned the car around and drove home slowly. When she got there, the people were gone and the house was quiet. She found an old Bible. The first verse she read as a new Christian was, "I have been crucified with Christ: and I myself no longer live, but Christ lives in me.

And the real life I now have within this body is a result of my trusting in the Son of God, who loved me and gave himself for me" (Gal. 2:20 LB). Was it mere chance that the Bible fell open to that verse?

Since that time, Judy's husband and children have given their lives to Jesus Christ. Her husband left his good job, and they moved out to Colorado. They left their wealthy friends and home, and now live on a ranch surrounded by a green valley and the majestic Rocky Mountains.

That day at the luncheon we gathered around Judy and laid our hands on her. Each of us prayed a simple prayer that Jesus would touch her ulcer and heal it. We pictured it gone. We prayed for complete healing of her body—mentally, physically, and emotionally.

A few weeks later, she was having surgery for another problem. The doctor decided that while he was operating, he should remove one-fourth of her stomach where the bleeding ulcer was. Old X rays indicated it was in such a position it could never heal. When the doctor prepared for that part of the operation, he discovered to his surprise that the ulcer was completely gone and only a small scar tissue was left. A complete healing had taken place!

I am often asked, "How should I pray for a loved one who is sick?" I believe we should always pray for complete healing unless God shows us otherwise, as in the case of my mother. I firmly believe that Jesus wants us to be well. He did not create sickness. It is the result of living in a sinful, fallen world. The fact that Jesus spent so much of His public ministry healing people should demonstrate to us that He doesn't want us to be sick. He wants us to be well. And He has given to us, as

Christians, the privilege of praying for the healing of others.

Why some are healed and others are not. This is a question with which we are often faced. I do not know why some people are healed and others are not. I do know that Christians must die, just as everyone else in the world must die. We do get sick. If Christians never got sick, there would be thousands of people turning to the Christian faith just so they would never get sick!

A businessman said to my husband recently, after the death of a friend, "I don't believe in this healing bit. God isn't in it. He doesn't heal one person and not the other. I don't think we should pray for healing."

How would you feel if you or your loved one were sick and your Christian friends wouldn't pray? What if they said, "It doesn't matter—what will be, will be!" I'll tell you how you would feel. You would feel exactly as I would—lost and alone, afraid and helpless, *without hope!*

Then think of the burden this would add to the one who was sick. No one praying for him or her! No hope! No spiritual comfort!

When Jesus heals a sick person, it is always for His honor and glory. It is always a testimony to the world of His power. Hundreds of people have been brought to Christ through seeing the miracle of His healing.

God uses the way Christians meet these trying situations as a testimony and witness to others. The singing of hymns in my mother's hospital room was a blessing to other patients and nurses.

He even uses the way we experience death to bring many to Himself. Over thirty-five people stood up and received Jesus as their Savior at a funeral of a Christian friend. These people had watched the way our young friend's wife had handled this experience. They saw the strength and peace that only Jesus could give, and, because of this, they are now members of God's family for all eternity!

How can we know what is really best in light of eternity? Our task is to be obedient to God, to His example, and to His command that we pray for one another when we are sick. We should pray for complete healing unless He shows us otherwise.

Helpful suggestions in praying for the sick:

(1) Always remember, Jesus is the One who heals. You do not heal anyone.

(2) When you pray for the healing of another, it is good to take one or two people with you who believe in the prayer of faith. If you do not feel you can pray in that situation with assurance and faith, find someone who can. Perhaps you should call for the minister and elders to anoint that person with oil and pray for them (James 5:14).

(3) Before you pray for the sick person, make sure you have asked God to show you *how* you should pray. The gift of wisdom and knowledge must go hand in hand with the prayer of healing.

(4) Try to find out (if the person is not unconscious) if there is anything in his life that would prevent the healing. Maybe he doesn't *really* want to get well. I know of a pastor's wife in a large church who cannot cope with the responsibilities that have been placed upon her. As a result, she has retreated behind a wall of illness; she does not want to be well.

Maybe he is holding bitterness or resentment in his heart. Explain these things to him and give him time to quietly confess anything the Holy Spirit brings to his mind. (If he should confess it in your hearing, you are honor-bound *before God* to hold it in confidence.)

(5) Read some passages from the Bible on healing. Share with him any stories of healing that would be helpful. This builds up the faith of the person who is sick as well as your own faith.

(6) Tell him to be open to receive the healing. For instance, he could say, "Thank You, Jesus, I receive Your healing into my life now." In praying for those who are ill, it is helpful to remember they will always be blessed through your prayer. They will be reminded again of God's deep love and care for them. And they will also feel a sense of your love and care. Sometimes they are healed, often they are improved, but they are *always* blessed.

Praying for your children:

(1) The one prayer I have prayed every day of my children's lives has been, "Lord, keep their hearts open and tender to the leading of Your Holy Spirit." And I have seen this prayer answered again and again.

Last week Harry and I and our son Tom and had a quiet candlelight dinner together. It was the first time we have been able to talk to Tom alone since he got home a few weeks ago. We no sooner had finished the prayer of thanksgiving than Tom began to ask Harry questions. It was almost as if he had been waiting all this time and couldn't wait another minute. After we had been talking for over two hours, Tom said, "You know, Dad, all I have been hearing for the past ten months is this other philosophy on nature and Eastern thinking. I needed to come home and hear the truth again from you. You are the only one I can talk to that I respect!" (How good the

Lord is! Harry had been so discouraged just a couple weeks ago, thinking he couldn't help his son!)

As the conversation passed into its third hour, there was an openness and tenderness about Tom that could only be through the Holy Spirit. Before he left that night, he said, "You and Mom have placed God right here in my heart from the time I was a little boy. And He has never left me. I will always be grateful to you for this, and I will always love you for it."

The one thing that has guarded Tom during these last five years is that his heart has been open and tender to the leading of the Holy Spirit. And this, ultimately, is what is going to bring him back to God's truth.

(2) To those of you who have small children at home, let me suggest that you go into their room at night while they are sleeping, lay your hands upon them, and pray. Pray that God will make of your children all He created them to be. If you know of a problem they are having, pray for it. If you see any disobedience in them, ask the Lord to remove it from their lives. Picture it leaving. There is a special value in praying for our children when they are asleep. Their spirits are at rest, and there isn't anything to distract them. I am told that mothers still do this in the small villages in England. It is a beautiful custom and one that has lasting value.

And your children don't have to be small for you to pray this way. Tom was experimenting with drugs several years ago while he was in college. I used to go into his room to wake him up every morning. Before I did, I would kneel down at the end of his bed, put my hands on his feet, and ask God to remove every desire for drugs from Tom's life. I pictured them leaving, and I pictured how he would look when his health was restored. I thanked God that His power was at work then in Tom's life. (I always reached for a pair of dirty socks in case he should wake up. Then I could say, "I'm just picking up the laundry!")

There isn't anything magical about laying your hands on a person, but it is biblical. There is something healing and comforting about the human touch. How often when our children are sick do we just reach out and touch them! Learn to pray this way for your children.

(3) Pray that God will surround your children (and your spouse and yourself) each day with His shield of protection. I picture a circle of light surrounding them, and nothing can get through that shield unless God permits it. I see Debbie walking down the hall at school with an invisible shield of God's protection all around her. When they're driving back and forth from college on the icy roads, I ask God to put an angel on each of the fenders and to surround the car with His shield of protection. And He does!

After Tom stopped experimenting with drugs, he was asked to go down to a small island off the coast of Texas to work for one summer. He was to get to know other young people on the beach and invite them to a small Bible study, which was held every night in a certain home. While he was there, a raging tropical hurricane hit the island. Everyone had to be evacuated. The students were put in one of the churches on the mainland. They were sitting on the floor across from a large plate-glass window, and Tom had just finished saying, "This hurricane doesn't seem too bad," when the roof of the church blew off and the plate-glass window blew in! Tom was sitting opposite the window, not even six feet away. The broken glass was flying at him, and he didn't even have time to move. All he could do was duck his head and try to protect himself with his arms.

After the glass had settled, the rest of the students said to him, "Tom, don't move! Just open your eyes and look." And when he opened his eyes, it was as though someone had drawn an invisible line within six inches all around him. Not one splinter of glass had crossed that line! When Tom told us about it later, he said, "Wow! It was just like there was a shield around me!" And I thought, "Thank You, Lord, there's that shield You put around my children, just like I pray for."

We may not always have such graphic illustrations of God's shield of protection, but just because we do not see it does not mean it isn't there. "Thou, O Lord, art a shield about me," the psalmist says. And He is.

(4) Pray for the future mates of your children. Start when they are babies or whatever age they are now. Pray for them several times a week. Pray that God will be with them wherever they are, that He will protect them from harm and danger and emotional problems. Pray that their hearts will be open to receiving the Lord Jesus as Savior when He is presented to them. Pray that God will bring them to your children at His timing and that He will bless their lives together.

Our daughter, Debbie, is engaged to be married this summer. I remember the first time we met Marc Gronholz. It was that happy Thanksgiving I told you about earlier in the book. The minute we met him, we felt as if he had always been part of the family. There was a feeling of love for him as though we had always known him. I'm sure it's because I have been praying for him every week for over twenty years!

Praying for your home. Go through your house, room

by room, and pray for it. Dedicate every part of it to the Lord. When you move into a new home or apartment, invite several Christian friends over and have a "house dedication." All of you go from room to room. Have an open Bible and read favorite passages. Pray that the blessing and power of the Holy Spirit will fill each room.

Maybe you would like to do this with just your family. Or if they do not want to do it, you can go through and pray for each room by yourself.

Pray that your home will be a lighthouse in this lost and dying world, that it will be a haven and a place of comfort and love to everyone who passes through it, especially your family. Pray that the love and peace of Jesus Christ will completely fill your home and every room in it. Pray that it will be a place where all honor and glory are given to Him.

"Now my eyes will be open and my ears attentive to the prayer that is made in this place. For now I have chosen and consecrated this house that my name may be there forever; my eyes and my heart will be there for all time" (2 Chron. 7:15, 16).

You can do the same thing if you live in a dormitory. You can also dedicate your business office to the Lord.

You may want to do this from time to time as the years pass.

GOD'S WORD

It would be impossible to close a book on prayer without mentioning, though briefly, the importance of reading God's Word, the Bible. You simply cannot separate prayer and the Bible. They must go hand-in-hand.

Imagine yourself arriving in heaven. Jesus and you are

walking down a shaded road together. Suddenly He turns to you and says, "By the way, how did you like the book I left you?" "Oh," you reply enthusiastically, "it was great, Lord. I carried it to church with me every Sunday, and it had the place of honor on the coffee table in our living room!" "That's fine," Jesus says, "But, tell Me, did you ever read it?" And you answer, "Well, no, Lord, I never did read it all the way through. But," you add hastily, "I used to read parts of it." Then Jesus looks at you sadly and says, "You mean you lived all those years on earth and never read My Book through once?"

So many of us today are up on all the latest Christian books. We never miss a one and can discuss them endlessly, but we spend so little time just reading God's Word.

Hudson Taylor told his son one day that he had just finished reading his Bible for the fortieth time in forty years! Do you wonder what made him such a great man of God?

Before you start your prayer of worship and intercession each day, sit down and read your Bible. Ask the Holy Spirit to open your heart to the truth He has for you that day.

SUGGESTIONS FOR BIBLE READING

(1) I suggest that you read the Bible through systematically. Don't skip around. Start with the Book of Genesis and, at the same time, with the Book of Acts and the Book of Matthew. Read one chapter each day in the Old Testament, one chapter in the New Testament, and one chapter in the Gospels. When you finish the four Gospels, start over again with Matthew. I don't think we can ever know the Gospels well enough.

(2) Read your Bible with a pencil in hand so you can mark any of the verses that speak to you. If there is a promise that seems meant just for you that day, jot down the date in the margin with a word or two as to how it met your need. This makes the Bible alive and personal to you.

(3) Put a *p* after every promise you read and a plus sign (+) after every command—something God says to do.

(4) Put a minus sign (-) after everything you are told not to do.

(5) Before closing your Bible, take a moment or two and say a prayer of thanksgiving over each thought you underlined.

You will find that as your Bible reading becomes a part of your daily prayer time, a whole new dimension will be added to your Christian life. Your time alone with God will become a time of power and spiritual renewal. You will discover that when you pray, Jesus' name is glorified in your life.

When you pray, life takes on new meaning and purpose; when you pray, you will see people come to Jesus; and when you pray, the power of God is made known to you and to the world. All God has waiting for us can only be acquired through prayer. There is no other way.

The tragedy of life is not *unanswered* prayer, but *unoffered* prayer.

"Always be full of joy in the Lord; I say it again, rejoice! Don't worry about anything; instead, *pray about everything*; tell God your needs and don't forget to thank him for his answers. If you do this you will experience God's peace, which is far more wonderful than the human mind can understand. His peace will keep your thoughts and your hearts quiet and at rest as you trust in Christ Jesus" (Phil. 4:4, 6, 7 LB, italics mine).

STUDY GUIDE

Respond fully and specifically to each of the following situations. Use Scripture references whenever possible.

1. Suppose a fellow believer tells you he has bought a little book entitled "Prayers for Each Day," which provides him with an adequate prayer life. Monday he prays the Monday prayer; Tuesday, the Tuesday prayer; and on through the week.

   What would you as a person who has just completed a study on prayer say to him? How would you clear up his misunderstanding and arouse enthusiasm for a more active prayer life?

2. Suppose a friend tells you he wants to have a more effective prayer life but doesn't know how to go about it. He tries to pray for a few minutes each day, but isn't consistent, and doesn't really know what to pray about. Actually, he admits that he feels a bit guilty about the whole thing.

   What counsel would you offer to your friend? What plans or methods would you suggest to help him seek a more effective and disciplined prayer life?

3. Supposing you have been praying fervently for money to purchase a much needed car (or whatever), and out of the blue, a member of your church calls and offers you a part-time job for two months that will give you the exact amount of money you need. You feel your prayer has been answered and happily

announce this news to your friends. But a skeptical friend says, "You would have gotten the job anyway. Prayer has nothing to do with it—you simply talked yourself into believing that God had something to do with a coincidence."

Without getting bent out of shape, how would you respond with a reasonable and authoritative answer?

4. Create a hypothetical situation of your own for personal research or to share with your study group.
5. Write out your own personal prayer using the nine steps as your guideline. Be as specific as possible. Share with your study group one thing that has been most helpful to you in this study on prayer.

OUTLINE

Note: Tear out this outline for your personal use or use it as you teach others to pray.

A. Arrow Prayers
B. Prayer of Worship and Intercession
   1. Make Time to Pray
   2. Find a Quiet Place
      a. Kneel.
      b. Pray out loud.
      c. Write down prayer requests.
   3. Say a Prayer of Protection
   4. Worship and Meditation
      a. Use psalms or hymns.
      b. Praise.
   5. Inner-Listening
      a. God brings to mind someone who needs prayer.
      b. Guidance is given on *what* to pray for and *how* to pray.
      c. Reveals unconfessed sin.
   6. Confession
      a. Be specific; name the sins.
      b. Move the sins that block God's channel of blessing.

7. The Prayer of Faith
   a. Mountains are moved through faith.
   b. God's "yes," "no," and "wait" answers.
8. Picture the Prayer as Answered
   a. How to use your creative imagination.
   b. We must pray; we must ask; we must believe.
   c. God's surprises.
9. Time of Thanksgiving
   a. Ask guidance on how to pray.
   b. Make your request.
   c. Make picture of prayer as answered.
   d. Thank God He is working now.

About the Authors

Hope MacDonald is a well-known speaker at retreats and churches throughout the country. She and her husband, Harry, live in Seattle, Washington, where Harry is senior pastor of the John Knox Presbyterian Church. They have three children and six grandchildren. She is the author of three other Zondervan books: *Discovering the Joy of Obedience*, *When Angels Appear*, and *The Flip Side of Liberation* (to be released in July 1990).

Dan MacDonald is the son of Hope and Harry. He is a graduate of Whitworth College and received his M. Div. degree from Conservative Baptist Seminary in Denver, Colorado. He was the chairman of the Bible department for nine years and taught Bible classes for nine years at Kings High School. He presently serves as pastor of the Community Christian Fellowship Church in Edmonds, Washington. Dan and his wife, Kathy, live in Lynnwood, Washington, with their two daughters.